77

# Professional French Pastry Series

Decorations, Borders and Letters,
Marzipan, and Modern Desserts

# Professional French Pastry Series

## Volume 4 :

## Decorations, Borders and Letters, Marzipan, and Modern Desserts

Roland Bilheux and Alain Escoffier

Under the direction of

Pierre Michalet

Translated by Rhona Poritzky-Lauvand and James Peterson

cicem

A copublication of
**CICEM** (Compagnie Internationale
de Consultation *Education* et *Media*)
**Paris**
**and**

**John Wiley & Sons, Inc.**
**New York • Toronto**

# Contents

# A Guide to French Pastry Making for the

**Basic Decorating Techniques**

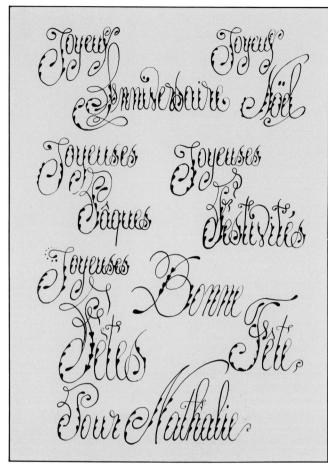

**Borders and Lettering**

## To know and to teach

This phrase characterizes the philosophy of the two authors, Roland Bilheux and Alain Escoffier

*The* Professional French Pastry Series *covers a wide range of skills that are useful not only to the pastry chef, but to restaurateurs and caterers.*

*Not only does the series cover the essentials to making the basic doughs encountered in traditional French pastry, but it also teaches the arts of confectionery, ice-cream making, chocolate work, pulling sugar, and a variety of other skills.*

*The restaurateur will find the Pro-fessional French Pastry Series ex-tremely valuable, not only for the preparation of desserts, but for any preparation calling for pastry, creams, and sorbets.*

*It will be equally helpful to caterers who are often called upon to prepare hors d'oeuvre and savory baked dishes.*

*The* Professional French Pastry Series *is a useful resource and refer-ence for anyone interested in learning more about French pastry, regardless of experience.*

# Beginner and Experienced Professional

**Modern Desserts**

**Sugar Work**

# The Professional French Pastry Series

**Diagram of Contents**

## Basic Pastry Preparations

| Basic doughs and batters | Basic creams | Basic Confectionery | Finished cakes |
|---|---|---|---|
| (Vol. 1) | (Vol. 2) | (Vol. 2) | (Vol. 2) |

## Assembled Pastries

| Assembled pastries | Finished cakes | Petits fours | Decorating techniques |
|---|---|---|---|
| Based on pâte brisée, pâte feuilletée, pâte levée (Vol. 2) | Finished products (Vol. 2 and Vol. 4) | (Vol. 3) | (Vol. 4) |

## Specialties

| Chocolate work | Ice-cream making | Sugar work | Modern specialties |
|---|---|---|---|
| Techniques and methods (Vol. 3) | Sorbets, ice creams, frozen desserts (Vol. 3) | All techniques (Vol. 3) | (Vol. 4) |

The **authors** of the *Professional French Pastry Series* are experienced **professionals** who are also **instructors** of pastry making at one of France's most prestigious government cooking schools.

The reader of the *Professional French Pastry Series,* whether an experienced professional or a beginner in the field, will find information applicable to all levels of French pastry making.

The text and photography in the four volumes of the *Professional French Pastry Series* was edited by **Pierre Michalet,** a specialist in educational materials. **Mr. Michalet** is the director of Editions Saint-Honoré.

# *Chapter 1*
# *Basic decorating techniques*

*A cake is good*

**A good-tasting** *cake is better*

**A good-tasting** *and* **good-looking** *cake is best!*

*A good-looking cake is a cake that has been well made and well decorated.*

*To make a good-looking cake, the pastry chef must master* **basic decorating techniques.**

*These techniques are introduced in this first chapter.*

# The finishing touches:

# the decoration!

11

# Basic decorating techniques:

Before beginning the decoration of a cake or other pastry, it is often necessary to prepare certain ingredients and equipment in advance. Many of the decorating techniques given in this volume are difficult, and if the equipment is not organized and readily at hand, success is less likely.

Here we have listed instructions particular to different ingredients.

## Adjusting the Color and Texture of Marzipan

A selection of colored marzipans that have already been adjusted to the right texture should be held in reserve. Otherwise, it will be necessary to work them at the last minute, which might overheat them and make them difficult to use.

## Coloring Marzipan

Marzipan is colored using government-approved food colorings. Any color can be used, with the intensities varied depending on final use. Pale colors are usually used for coating entire cakes, while brighter colors are used for flowers.

It is important to use the most concentrated food colorings available for dying marzipan. If the coloring is too dilute, it will thin the marzipan and make it difficult to work with.

Use a small amount of coloring at a time; otherwise it is easy to add too much, making the marzipan too bright. If too much coloring is added to a batch of marzipan, some plain marzipan can be worked into the colored batch to lighten it.

## Mixing Marzipans

There are two possibilities:
- A partial combination of two different-colored marzipans, to give a streaked, marbled effect to the finished product. This technique is hard to control, and the result is not always predictable.
- A complete combination of two different batches of marzipan. This requires working the marzipan several times on the work surface to obtain an evenly colored mass. The long working tends to warm and soften the marzipan.

*Note*

When chocolate marzipan is needed, it should be colored and flavored with cocoa powder.

Secondary colors are usually obtained by combining several different batches of marzipan that have already been colored.

## Consistency of the Marzipan

Marzipan should have a firm consistency without being brittle. If it is too dry, it tends to develop cracks and split while being rolled. If, on the other hand, the marzipan is too soft, it sticks while being rolled and loses its shape when applied to finished pastries.

## Adjusting the Consistency

Marzipan is at the correct consistency when a rose prepared from it remains firm at room temperature. The petals should remain whole and not tear while being rolled, nor should the rose petals droop once the rose is set on the finished pastry.

If the marzipan is too hard and dry, it can be worked through a grinder or worked on a marble by hand with a few drops of liquor or glucose.

If the marzipan is brittle, the same technique can be used, but instead, add a piece of fondant the size of a walnut to 1 kg (35 oz.) of the paste.

If the marzipan is too soft, it can be worked on a pastry marble with a little bit of powdered milk or a mixture of equal parts powdered milk and cornstarch. Work the dry ingredients progressively into the almond paste until the right consistency is achieved.

*Important*

Never allow a crust to form on the surface of marzipan. To prevent this, make sure that it is tightly sealed in plastic wrap during storage. Once a crust has formed on the surface of marzipan, it must be reground in a mechanical grinder.

## Adjusting the Consistency of Butter Cream

The final consistency of butter cream is adjusted immediately before it is used. This is necessary because butter cream reacts to slight changes in the temperature and humidity of the work area. Final adjustments are almost always needed.

The desired consistency of butter cream depends on its final use:

- **Stiff:** for decorating with a pastry bag. Stiffness is needed to ensure that the decoration stays in place and maintains its shape.

- **Soft:** for covering cakes and other preparations. The butter cream should be soft enough to spread evenly.

- **Runny:** for glazing certain preparations (see volume 2). The butter cream should be slowly heated and worked with a spatula until it is almost liquid and perfectly smooth.

# preparation of the ingredients

If a batch of butter cream has been contaminated with crumbs from cakes, pieces of nuts, or other particles, it should be strained through a fine-mesh drum sieve before being used.

These particles would not only be visible on the surface of a finished cake, but would clog the pastry bag.

Avoid using too much alcoholic flavoring in butter creams, as they can become too thin, as well as break up. If a butter cream breaks or becomes grainy, it can be brought back together by adding a small amount of melted clarified butter.

**Preparing Ingredients for Final Decoration**

Make sure that all the ingredients used to coat or decorate a cake, such as toasted almonds, slivered almonds, cake crumbs, and the like, have been prepared in advance and stored in airtight containers.

It is also advisable to prepare other special decorating materials, such as chocolate shavings or chocolate cigarettes (see volume 3) in advance.

# La glace royale (Royal icing)

## Uses

Royal icing can be used both cooked and raw: for glazing certain pastries such as conversations, jésuites, and allumettes, and for decorating sucre au rocher (rock sugar). It can also be used for decorations applied with a pastry bag, paper cone, or pastry brush.

Royal icing is rarely flavored but is often dyed with food coloring.

Because royal icing is only occasionally used and quickly loses its consistency, it is prepared as it is needed, especially when used for decorations applied with a paper cone.

## Equipment

Mixing bowl and paddle attachment for electric mixer or
Stainless steel, glass, or plastic mixing bowl
Wooden spatula
Plastic pastry scraper
Wet towel or plastic wrap
Measuring cup
Fine-mesh strainer
Clean sheet of parchment paper
Bowl for separating eggs

## Recipe

For 1 egg white, use 150 g (5 oz.) sifted confectioners' sugar and several drops of lemon juice or vinegar (optional).

## Preparation

Depending on the intended use of the royal icing, certain precautions should be followed during and after its preparation. If the royal icing is to be used for decoration, it should be fine and perfectly smooth. If there are any grains or particles in the icing, they will clog the tip of the paper cone, possibly spoiling the decoration.

The egg whites should be strained through a fine-mesh strainer before being combined with the sugar. This straining will eliminate any particles of umbilical cord or shell that would clog the paper cone.

The confectioners' sugar should be carefully sifted, preferably through a fine-mesh drum sieve, before being weighed. In France, special sieves are available for this purpose.

If lemon juice is being used, make sure that all particles of pulp and, of course, seeds are eliminated.

For certain applications of royal icing, such as glazing the surface of conversations and allumettes, the above precautions are not necessary, as a paper cone is not used.

## Procedure

When making small quantities of royal icing, weighing fractions of single egg whites is very difficult. It is thus almost impossible to calculate the amount of sugar that will be needed. When preparing small quantities, it is therefore best to work by eye. If working with larger quantities, such as four whites, 125 ml (4.5 fl. oz.), it is best to weigh the ingredients using the proportions given above.

Place the egg whites in a mixing bowl or the bowl of an electric mixer. Make sure the bowl is perfectly clean. Add three-fourths of the sugar called for to the whites.

> The preparation of royal icing is straightforward and presents few difficulties. Pay careful attention to the smoothness and final consistency. Make sure that a crust is not allowed to form on the surface before application.

When beginning the mixing, it is best to work by hand with a wooden spatula or with the electric mixer set at slow speed. This prevents the sugar from blowing around and spattering on the sides of the bowl.

Once the ingredients have been combined, beat more quickly either by hand or with the mixer. Be sure to scrape the sides of the bowl from time to time with the plastic pastry scraper so that no undissolved grains of sugar remain in the icing.

Continue to beat the icing until it is perfectly smooth and has the desired consistency. If the icing is too thin, add as much of the remaining sugar as necessary to achieve the right consistency.

A few drops of lemon juice or vinegar added at the end will give the royal icing a whiter appearance but will also cause it to form a crust.

Royal icing should always be energetically beaten just before being used. This

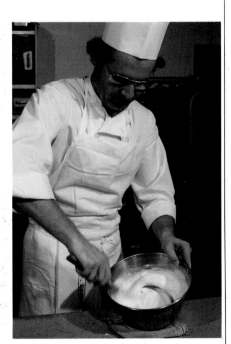

makes it lighter in both color and texture and gives it the desired ribbon-forming consistency.

### Adjusting the Consistency

The final consistency of the royal icing can be adjusted, depending on its eventual use.

If it is to be applied with a paper cone, its consistency should be adjusted in the same way as pâte à choux (see volume 1, pages 50 to 53).

If the royal icing is to be used for glazing, it should be relatively stiff. It can be made stiffer by adding a small

amount of flour or cornstarch, which will help it to hold up in the oven.

Once the royal icing has been adjusted to the proper consistency, carefully scrape the sides of the bowl and cover with a wet towel or plastic wrap to prevent a crust from forming on the surface.

If a crust forms, the icing cannot be applied with a paper cone.

### Storage

If well covered, royal icing should maintain its consistency for up to 6 hours. Because of its sensitivity to air, it should be prepared the day it is needed.

If any royal icing is left over, it can be stored in the refrigerator, well covered with plastic or a wet towel.

Royal icing that has been stored for longer than 6 hours should be vigorously beaten just before being put into the paper cone in order to restore some of its fluidity.

In any case, leftover royal icing never works as well as fresh icing. Royal icing cannot be stored for long periods, as it tends to break and become too runny.

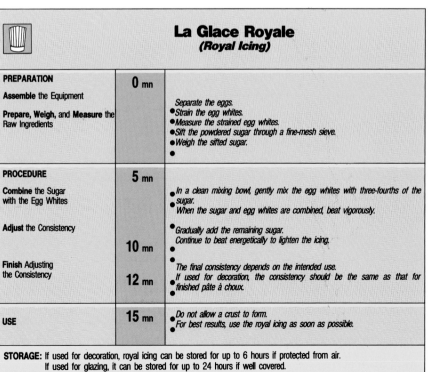

## La Glace Royale
### (Royal Icing)

| PREPARATION | 0 mn | |
|---|---|---|
| **Assemble** the Equipment | | Separate the eggs. |
| **Prepare, Weigh,** and **Measure** the Raw Ingredients | | • Strain the egg whites. <br> • Measure the strained egg whites. <br> • Sift the powdered sugar through a fine-mesh sieve. <br> • Weigh the sifted sugar. <br> • |
| PROCEDURE | 5 mn | |
| **Combine** the Sugar with the Egg Whites | | • In a clean mixing bowl, gently mix the egg whites with three-fourths of the sugar. <br> • When the sugar and egg whites are combined, beat vigorously. |
| **Adjust** the Consistency | 10 mn | • Gradually add the remaining sugar. <br> Continue to beat energetically to lighten the icing. <br> • |
| **Finish Adjusting** the Consistency | 12 mn | The final consistency depends on the intended use. <br> • If used for decoration, the consistency should be the same as that for finished pâte à choux. |
| USE | 15 mn | • Do not allow a crust to form. <br> • For best results, use the royal icing as soon as possible. |

**STORAGE:** If used for decoration, royal icing can be stored for up to 6 hours if protected from air.
If used for glazing, it can be stored for up to 24 hours if well covered.

# Le cacao décor (Chocolate icings)

## Introduction

Chocolate decoration was first used by Antonin Carême at the beginning of the nineteenth century. It was Carême who invented the modern style of pastry decoration and presentation.

Usually, unsweetened cooa powder is added to a decorating base to give it a dark brown color. The mixture is then applied to finished cakes and pastries with a paper cone or pastry brush.

These cocoa-based mixtures are often used instead of melted covering chocolate for decoration because of certain distinct advantages:

- Cocoa-based mixtures are darker than regular chocolate and stand out better against colored backgrounds.
- It is easier to adjust the color and consistency of cocoa-based mixtures.
- Cocoa-based mixtures are less sensitive to changes in temperature and hold their consistency better.
- Cocoa-based mixtures are less expensive.

## Equipment

### Method A

Fine-mesh drum sieve, clean sheet of parchment paper, mixing bowl, whisk, plastic pastry scraper, fine-mesh strainer, saucepan for the syrup, measuring cup 1-L (1-qt.) plastic container with tight-fitting lid

### Method B

Mixing bowl
Fine-mesh strainer
Saucepan for the syrup
Plastic pastry scraper
1-L (1-qt.) plastic container with tight-fitting lid

## Recipes

### Recipe A (cocoa powder)

125 g shortening (4.5 oz.)
175 g cocoa powder (6 oz.)
500 ml sugar syrup (17 fl. oz.), at 1260 D, consisting of:
　250 ml water (8.5 fl. oz.)
　250 g sugar (9 oz.)
　125 g glucose (4.5 oz.)

### Recipe B (bitter chocolate in squares)

300 g good-quality bitter chocolate (10.5 oz.)
500 ml sugar syrup (17 fl. oz.), at 1260 D, consisting of:
　250 ml water (8.5 fl. oz.)
　250 g sugar (9 oz.)
　125 g glucose (4.5 oz.)

## Preparation

There are several recipes and many methods for preparing chocolate-based decorating mixtures. All use either cocoa powder or bitter chocolate in squares. Sweet or semisweet chocolate is never used.

Because the icing is heated during its preparation, it is often convenient to prepare it in advance or even the day before.

When the mixture is still warm, it tends to be quite liquid. It stiffens as it cools.

## Procedure

### Method A: Cocoa Powder

Prepare the sugar syrup, taking the usual precautions (see volume 2, pages 14 to 17).

In a small, clean mixing bowl, melt the shortening. Stir in the cocoa powder in two stages with a whisk. The mixture should be perfectly smooth.

To this mixture, add 300 ml (10 fl. oz.) of the hot sugar syrup. Be sure that the sugar syrup has been strained before adding it to the chocolate mixture. Stir

 Chocolate icing is simple to prepare, but certain precautions should be closely followed : the ingredients should be at the correct temperatures ; all the equipment should be clean and dry ; the raw ingredients should be of the best quality

the mixture with a whisk until it is smooth. The mixture will stiffen because of the formation of an emulsion of chocolate, particles of fat, and water. It is this stiffening that gives the mixture the desired consistency.

Carefully scrape the sides of the bowl with a plastic pastry scraper. Transfer the chocolate decorating mixture into a container that has a tight-fitting lid.

While the mixture is cooling, cover the container with a moist towel, not the lid, to allow cooling but prevent particles and dust from falling in. Once the mixture has cooled, put on the lid. Make sure that the container is well sealed.

*Important*

The temperature of the ingredients should be checked before they are combined. The shortening should be between 50° and 60°C (122° and 140°F) before being mixed with the cocoa powder. The cocoa powder should be at room temperature. The sugar syrup should be from 70° to 80°C (160° to 175°F).

### Method B: Unsweetened Chocolate in Squares

Be sure to select a good-quality

unsweetened chocolate when using this method. Bring the sugar syrup to a simmer. Skim off any froth that floats to the surface.

While the syrup is heating, chop the chocolate into small chunks and place it in a bowl large enough to contain both the chocolate and sugar syrup.

Strain the hot syrup, 80°C (175°F), over the chopped chocolate. Stir quickly with a whisk until all the chocolate has melted. Continue stirring until the mixture is smooth. The quantity of chocolate

may need to be adjusted to a given amount of syrup. If the icing seems too thin, more chocolate can be added.

Place the mixture in a clean container with a tight-fitting lid. Follow the same cooling instructions as for method A.

### Storage

The chocolate decorating mixture can be stored in the refrigerator, 5°C (40°F), for several weeks.

### Reusing Leftover Icing

Take the mixture out of the refrigerator as it is needed.

Bring the mixture to room temperature by leaving it out, or gently warm it in a double boiler until it attains the desired consistency.

*Note:*

When heating the chocolate mixture, make sure to use a perfectly clean and dry container. Work it as little as possible during the reheating; overworking can cause the fat to separate and the mixture to break.

The correct consistency for chocolate decorating mixture is the same as that for fondant used to glaze pâte à choux pastries (see volume 2, pages 128 to 131).

| Le Cacao Décor (Chocolate Icing, cocoa powder method) | | |
|---|---|---|
| **PREPARATION** | **0** min | |
| **Assemble** the Equipment | | • Remember to use a clean container for storing the mixture. • All equipment should be perfectly clean and dry. |
| **Prepare, Weigh, and Measure** the Raw Ingredients | | • Sift the cocoa through a fine-mesh drum sieve onto a clean sheet of parchment paper. |
| **PROCEDURE** | **5** min | |
| **Prepare** the Sugar Syrup | | • Boil the syrup for 1 minute. |
| **Melt** the Shortening | | • Use a bain-marie (double boiler). • Use a perfectly clean and dry mixing bowl. |
| **Add** the Cocoa Powder | **10** min | • Gently stir the cocoa powder into the shortening with a whisk until smooth. • Add the cocoa powder in two stages. |
| **Add** the Sugar Syrup | **11** min | • The syrup should be at 80°C (175°F) and strained. |
| **Smooth** the Mixture | **12** min | • Stir with a whisk until the mixture is perfectly smooth. |
| **TRANSFERRING THE MIXTURE** | | • Put the finished mixture into a clean container; cover with a wet towel until cool, then cover with a tight-fitting lid. |
| **STORAGE:** The mixture will keep for several weeks in the refrigerator, 5°C (40°F). | | |

# Les glaçages et nappages
# (Icings, glazes, and coatings)

A large number of cakes are either entirely or partially iced or glazed.

The final icing of a cake is an extremely important aspect of its decoration, regardless of the type of icing used.

The final icing on a cake or pastry contributes to the finished product in three ways:

1. If the icing is an integral part of the recipe, it is usually chosen to harmonize with the other components of the finished product. Examples are fondant on napoleons, apricot or neutral glaze on fruits and fruit desserts, and fruit or chocolate icing used to reinforce the flavor of certain pastries and cakes.

2. The icing or glaze contributes sheen and a clean look to finished pastries. It gives the pastries a finished, professional appearance.

3. Icings and glazes help protect cakes and other pastries by forming a seal that is impermeable to air and moisture. This helps the pastries keep longer without drying out or taking on disagreeable flavors.

# The Different Icings

## A. Fondant-based icing

## B. Fruit-preserve/jelly-based glazes

## C. Fruit-coulis-based glazes

## D. Chocolate icings and coatings

## A. Fondant-based Icings

The correct adjustment of the consistency and temperature of fondant is essential. See Filling and Glazing Pâte à Choux–based Pastries in volume 2, pages 128 to 131.

**Note**

When working in areas with high humidity (during storms, in tropical climates, near the ocean, for example) about 10 percent glucose or 5 percent clarified butter can be added to the fondant to improve its appearance and help it to hold up.

This will also help prevent the fondant from dripping or becoming runny once it is applied to the finished pastries.

# B. Fruit-preserve/jelly-based Glazes

Fruit preserve glazes are usually applied with a pastry brush. Their consistency and temperature are best adjusted by gradually heating them on top of the stove. They should not be overworked during the heating, as this tends to eliminate some of their sheen.

Fruit-preserved-based glazes and coatings are best applied at 70° to 80°C (160° to 175°F). Their consistency is best adjusted by adding fruit juice or sugar syrup at 1260 D. Sometimes vanilla extract, fruit flavoring, or an appropriate liquor or liqueur is added.

Clear jellies can be prepared as glazes in the same way as preserves, but they are usually used at a lower temperature, 40° to 60°C (105° to 140°F).

Check the consistency of the glaze by pouring a few drops onto a plate. The glaze should be gelatinous without being too sticky.

A colorless jelly is sometimes used. It has the advantage of letting the natural color of the fruit shine through. It is prepared by bringing 1 L (34 fl. oz.) of sugar syrup at 1260 D to a simmer with 15 to 20 g (1/2 to 2/3 oz.) of pectin. Colorless jelly can be flavored with different fruit flavors.

# C. Fruit-coulis-based Glazes

These glazes are combinations of fruit coulis, sugar syrup at 1260 D, and gelatin or pectin. They are more fragile and perishable than fruit-preserve-based glazes. They are mainly used to reinforce the flavor of the fruit contained in certain pastries and cakes. They are sometimes served as sauces to accompany various cakes and pastries (see volume 2, pages 79 to 80).

# D. Chocolate Icings and Coatings

**There are three categories of chocolate icings and coatings:**

1. **Liquid covering chocolate (couverture)**
2. **Sprayed glazes**
3. **Ganaches**

## 1. Liquid Covering Chocolate (Couverture)

These coatings are prepared by combining dark or milk chocolate with cocoa butter and vegetable oil.

1 kg couverture chocolate (35 oz.)
50 g cocoa butter (1.5 oz.)
80 to 120 ml vegetable oil (3 to 4 fl. oz.) —the amount of oil depends on the desired consistency of the coating

# E. Fondant- and Preserve-based Coatings Containing Glucose

### Uses

Decorating mixtures often contain food coloring. Depending on the style of pastry and decoration, these mixtures can be based on fondant or fruit preserves and jellies.

For either of these mixtures, it is helpful to add glucose, as it makes them more supple and elastic and hence easier to work with. Glucose also contributes to the final sheen and helps bring out the natural color of the cake or pastry.

### Fondant/Glucose Decorating Mixture

1 part white fondant, worked until malleable
1 part glucose

Heat the mixture and work it until the ingredients are well combined.

When coloring the mixture to use for flowers, make the colors quite bright.

### Fruit Preserve/Glucose Decorating Mixture

2 parts fruit preserves or fruit glaze
1 part glucose

Gently heat the ingredients and stir them until they are smooth and well combined.

Strain the mixture through a drum sieve or fine-mesh strainer to remove any particles, which would clog the paper cone during the decoration.

This mixture can then be tinted with food coloring if desired.

### Note

Both of the above mixtures should be gently warmed before application to cakes and pastries.

## 2. Sprayed Glazes

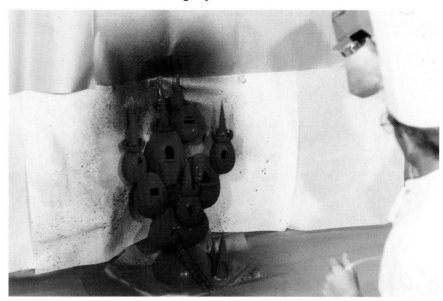

Glazing with a spray gun makes it possible to apply a thin coating of chocolate to finished pastries. Even though spraying is a recent development, it produces all the necessary characteristics of classic glazes and coatings.

It gives a finished, professional appearance to pastries, contributes to their final flavor, and protects them from air and moisture. A spray gun is required (see volume 3, Decorating with a Spray Gun, page 70).

## 3. Ganaches for Coating

(see volume 2, pages 46 to 47 and 124 to 125).

Chocolate ganache can be prepared with either dark covering chocolate (couverture), semisweet chocolate, milk chocolate, or white chocolate. Usually the chocolate is combined with an equal quantity of milk or cream, 1 kg chocolate to 1 L milk or heavy cream (35 oz. chocolate to 34 fl. oz. milk or heavy cream).

Ganache used for masking and coating cakes should not be whipped and should be applied at 30° to 35°C (85° to 95°F).

> The preparation of chocolate icings and coatings is straightforward and requires no special knowledge or techniques. These icings and coatings should be used while slightly warm.

| La Ganache de Glaçage<br>*(Ganaches for Coating)* | | |
|---|---|---|
| **PREPARATION**<br><br>**Assemble** the Equipment<br><br>**Prepare, Weigh, and Measure** the Raw Ingredients | **0** min | • *Measure the milk or cream.*<br>• *Chop the chocolate into chunks.* |
| **PROCEDURE**<br>**Heat** the Milk<br><br>**Add** the Milk<br><br>**Stir** the Mixture<br><br><br>Cool | **3** min<br><br><br><br>**5** min | • *Bring the milk to a simmer on the stove.*<br>• *Pour the simmering milk over the chopped chocolate.*<br>• *Stir with a whisk until the mixture is smooth and the chocolate is completely melted.*<br>• *Let the ganache cool at room temperature. Stir it from time to time while it is cooling.* |
| **APPLICATION** | **30** min | • *The ganache should be applied to cakes and pastries while slightly warm.* |
| **STORAGE:** Ganache will keep for several days in the refrigerator, 5°C (40°F). It should be gently reheated before use. | | |

# Coating cakes and pastries

This is the easiest and most direct method for decorating cakes and pastries. It consists of partially or completely coating the surface of the cake or pastry with an appropriate ingredient such as chopped almonds or chocolate sprinkles.

The surface of the pastry or cake to be coated should still be soft and moist rather than crusty. If a hard crust has formed, the coating will not adhere.

The coating should be applied as evenly as possible and pressed onto the surface of the pastry with a metal spatula or the side of a large knife.

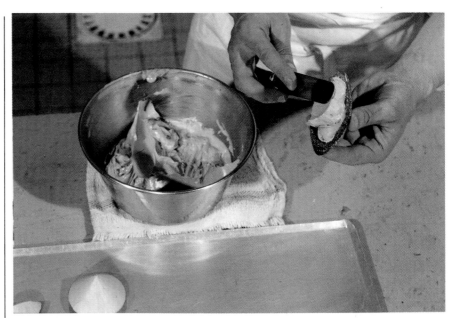

### Partial Coating

When a cake is partially coated, it is imperative that the edges of the coating be perfectly even. If only the sides of a cake are being coated, make sure the coating extends exactly to the top all around the cake. The same holds true if the coating is being applied only halfway up the sides of the cake. Make sure the line where the coating ends is even.

### Using a Stencil

An infinite variety of shapes can be cut out of cardboard and used as templates or stencils for decorating cakes. Usually the stencil or template is placed on the surface of the cake and the coating element sprinkled over. The stencil is then removed, and the design is left on the top of the cake. It is, of course, possible to cut out stencils in reverse so that the background is coated rather than the design.

# Decorating with a pastry bag

*The pastry bag is often used for decorating cakes and pastries. Butter cream is most often used, but other mixtures also can be used.*

*Even though some pastry chefs consider this technique somewhat old-fashioned, it is a necessary part of a professional chef's repertoire. The ability to use the pastry bag to decorate the surfaces of cakes and pastries offers a wide range of possibilities for decoration. It also allows the pastry chef to invent and personalize his or her cakes.*

*Four types of icings or creams can be used for decorating with a pastry bag:*

*1. Butter cream*

*2. Ganache*

*3. Chantilly cream*

*4. Italian meringue*

23

# 1. Decorating with butter cream

## Special Techniques

Butter cream offers the pastry chef a wide range of decorating possibilities for cakes and pastries.

One technique that lends a nice touch to the decoration is to fill each side of the pastry bag with a different colored butter cream, for example, coffee on one side and chocolate on the other.

Many pastry chefs like to combine different techniques to decorate the same cake. Part of the design can be executed using a pastry bag with a small fluted tip. The fine details are then filled in using a paper cone.

## Technical Recommendations

Always use butter cream that is soft and easy to work. If it is too firm, work it until it attains the correct consistency.

Be very careful when using the pastry bag. Make sure that it is perfectly clean and that the inside is free of odors. Rinse it with hot water if necessary.

Do not put too much butter cream in the pastry bag. This is especially true with decoration that requires considerable dexterity. A large pastry bag filled with butter cream is awkward to use.

Place the cake near the edge of the work surface, preferably on a stiff piece of cardboard or other material. This makes the cake easier to move about and keep within easy reach.

Make sure the surface of the cake is perfectly smooth and neat before beginning the decoration.

Before beginning the actual decoration, the pastry chef should have a clear idea of how he or she is going to proceed. The decoration should be approached systematically. It is best to decorate the outside border first, then locate and decorate the exact center of the cake. Once the border and center are decorated, they can serve as reference points for finishing the rest of the cake.

# 2. Decorating with ganache

Follow the recommendations given for working with butter cream.

# Woven decorations using a fluted tip

This technique is primarily used for decorating strips of cake or pastries that are to be sold in pastry shops by the piece. Two tips are required for the decoration: a plain no. 7 and a flat, fluted tip. The flat tip can be purchased or made by pressing together the tines of a regular fluted tip.

### Technical Recommendations

Use two different-colored butter creams. Make sure they have the right consistency.

Check the condition of the tips and pastry bags.

Pipe one of the butter creams in strips to divide the cake into even sections, using the no. 7 plain tip.

With the flat, fluted tip, pipe a strip of the other butter cream over every other lateral strip. Repeat this operation four times in alternating rows. Continue until the entire surface of the cake is covered with an even, decorative pattern.

*Note*

Even though this page and those that follow are devoted to using the pastry bag to decorate with the four creams

and icings mentioned on page 27, fluted tips for pastry bags can be used for a much wider variety of fillings and creams.

Examples are the special cream filling used for Paris-Brests, mousseline cream, chocolate whipped cream, and pastry cream.

Once the pastry chef has worked in the profession for several years, the almost innumerable uses of the pastry bag and its various tips will become almost automatic.

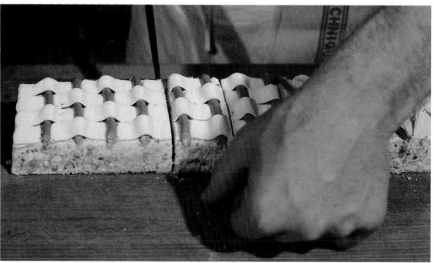

# Examples of cakes decorated with butter cream

# Examples of cakes decorated

# with butter cream

# Examples of cakes decorated

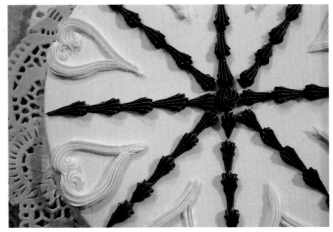

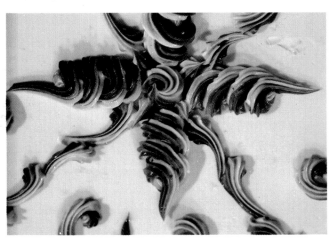

# with butter cream

# 3. Decorating with Chantilly cream

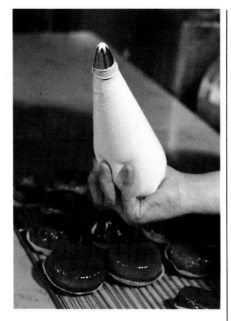

When decorating with Chantilly cream, a medium to large fluted tip should be used. Chantilly cream is used to decorate three types of preparations:

- cakes, frozen desserts, and fruit tarts (strawberry tart)

- special desserts such as vacherins, Saint-Honoré, and chocolate timbales

- savarins, babas, and pâte à choux desserts such as swans and baskets

All the illustrated designs made with butter cream can be made with Chantilly cream as well.

To pipe Chantilly cream with a pastry bag, follow the recommendations for decorating with butter cream:

- Avoid overfilling the pastry bag.

- Check to make sure the pastry tips are in good condition before attaching them to the pastry bag.

- Place the cake to be decorated on a stiff piece of cardboard or other material near the edge of the work surface. This makes it easier to decorate and move the cake without damaging it.

- Be clear about the decoration and proceed in a systematic way.

# 4. Decorating with Italian meringue

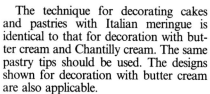

The technique for decorating cakes and pastries with Italian meringue is identical to that for decoration with butter cream and Chantilly cream. The same pastry tips should be used. The designs shown for decoration with butter cream are also applicable.

*Important*

When cakes and pastries are decorated with Italian meringue, they are usually placed for a short time in a hot oven or under a broiler to color the meringue.

When using this technique, it is best to apply the decoration at the last minute and to sprinkle it with powdered sugar before the final browning.

# Decorating with a knife

Certain pastries, usually those based on puff pastry (*pâte feuilletée*), can be decorated by making incisions with a knife.

The main purpose for making incisions on the surfaces of pastries is to create an appealing decorative effect. Several types of incisions can be made, ranging from simple to quite complex.

Knife cuts on the surface of a pastry should be made so that they open and expand evenly in the oven.

Usually a small paring knife is used to make the incisions in the pastry. It should be extremely sharp so that the cut can be made without going all the way through the pastry. Avoid making cuts completely through the pastry. When working with the paring knife, it is best to hold it by the blade between the thumb and index finger. The handle of the knife is not gripped but should float freely within the palm of the hand.

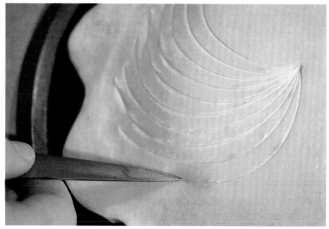

The knife should be held at a 45-degree angle in relation to the pastry being decorated. This angle should be maintained in two directions:

a. The blade of the knife should be held over the pastry at a 45-degree angle lengthwise.

b. The blade of the knife should be held at a sideways angle of 45 degrees over the pastry so that the cut is actually made into the pastry from the side.

Cutting decorative streaks into pastries can at times be quite a delicate operation.

This is especially true for apple turnovers (chaussons aux pommes), where the pastry is often of irregular thickness and has an irregular surface, so that it is easy to cut all the way through the dough.

Be especially careful that difficult, irregularly shaped pastries are well chilled so that the dough is as firm as possible.

When sliding the blade of the knife over the pastry, be sure to hold it in a relaxed way so that it can follow the contours.

Some of the more elaborate, fanciful knife decorations require considerable dexterity. This is particularly true with galettes des rois.

*Note:* Some pastries such as the Pithiviers have a prescribed knife decoration that should be used (see volume 2, Pithiviers, pages 195 to 196).

# Prepared decorations for cakes

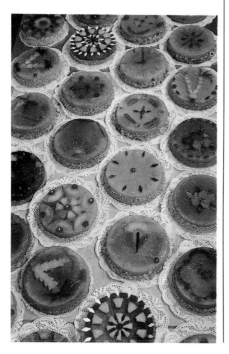

**Five decorating elements are prepared separately and later added to cakes for decoration.**

**Candied fruits** (see volume 2, pages 90 to 91): Because of the wide variety of candied fruits that are available to the pastry chef, they can be used in an almost infinite number of ways.

**Pastillage** (see volume 3, pages 167 to 169): Pastillage is occasionally used in a limited way to decorate the surfaces of certain cakes and pastries.

**Chocolate** (see volume 3, pages 37 to 71): A wide variety of chocolate decorations can be prepared separately and placed on the surfaces of cakes and pastries.

**Nougatine** (see volume 2, pages 108 to 111): Nougatine is sometimes used for decorating cakes and pastries, but consideration should be given to the time required for its preparation.

**Royal icing** (see pages 18 to 19, this volume): Royal icing is sometimes used to make designs, which are first dried either at room temperature or in a proof box before being applied.

# Decorating with candied fruits

In decoration, candied fruits are mainly used for fruit-based cakes.

The fruits can be cut into different shapes and used to form designs.

Several colors and fruits can be used on the same cake, but restraint should be exercised. Never have more than three or four colors on top of the same cake.

Cut the candied fruits as evenly as possible and arrange them carefully on the surface of the cake.

If the fruits are carelessly arranged, these cakes can look very amateurish and unappealing.

# Examples of cakes decorated

# with candied fruits

# Examples of cakes decorated

# with candied fruits

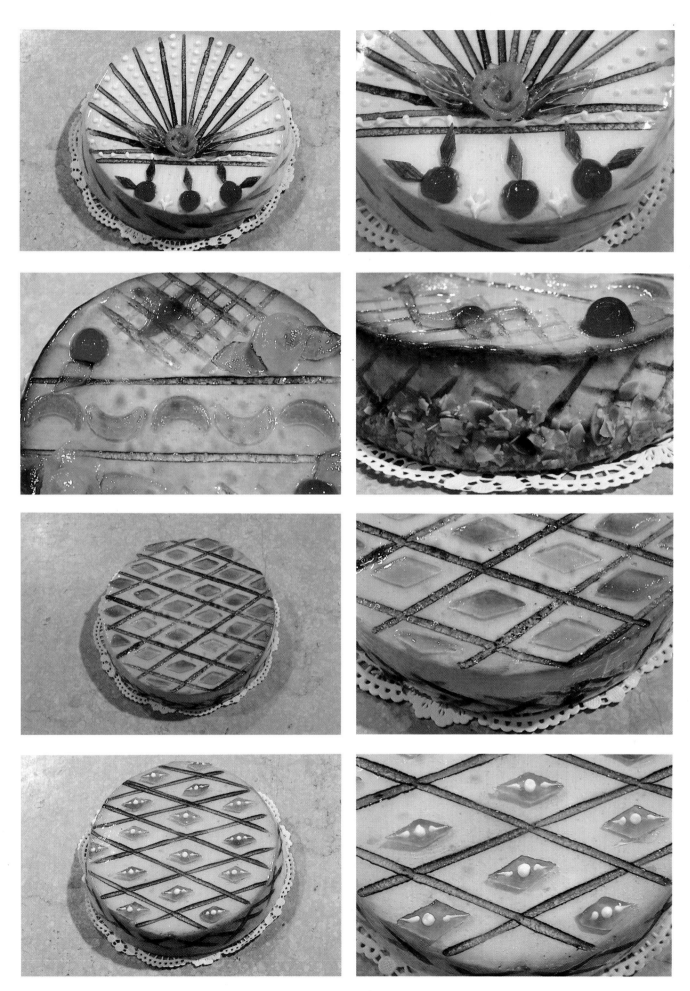

# Decorating a fruit cake

# Decorating with nougatine

# Examples of royal icing designs

Premade royal icing designs are often used in pastry making. They can be made in advance so that they are immediately available when needed. They are used on a variety of pastries, including petits fours and individual cakes. They are prepared by piping royal icing onto thick plastic sheets with a paper cone. They are then allowed to dry at room temperature or in a proof box.

Below are several examples. The technique can be used for any type of design, depending on the whim of the pastry chef.

Royal icing designs can also be prepared in different colors. The coloring is added either by dying the royal icing with food coloring or by airbrushing the finished designs with food coloring. Once the royal icing designs have completely dried, they should be stored in tight-fitting containers and protected from air and moisture.

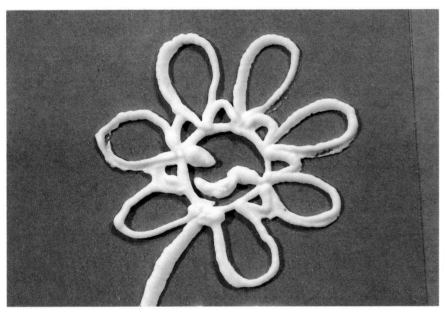

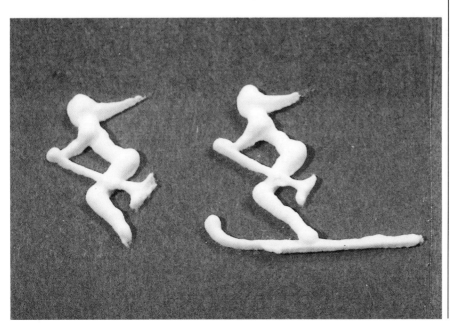

# Examples of royal icing designs

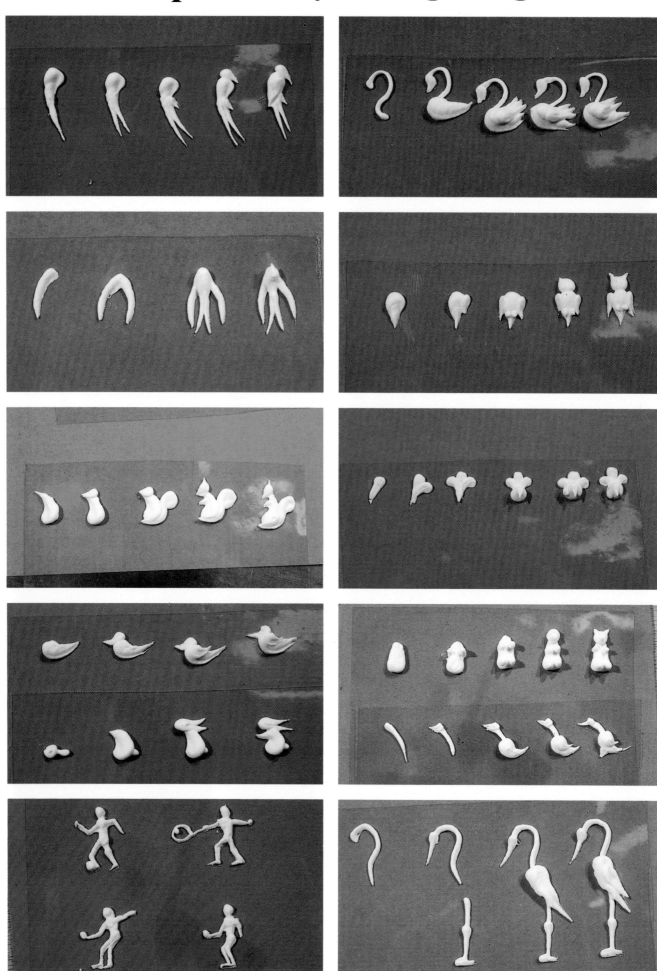

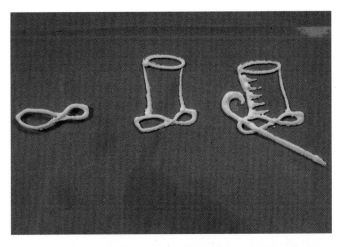

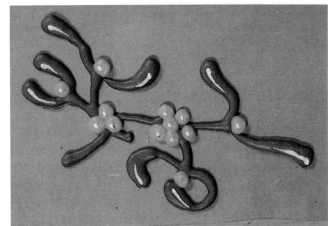

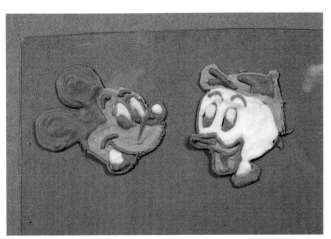

# Decorating with a paper cone

## Introduction

*In many ways, decorating desserts with a paper cone is similar to using the pastry bag. The primary difference is that the paper cone is miniature, is made out of stiff paper, and is made anew for each use. Paper cones are discarded after use.*

*A paper cone is most often used for writing or drawing elaborate designs on the surfaces of cakes.*

The paper cone (cornet) is one of the most useful tools available to the pastry chef. It is used for the most refined types of decoration.

**The paper cone is the pastry chef's fountain pen**

Every beginning pastry chef should realize the importance of mastering the use of the paper cone.

It is a technique that should be developed from the beginning of the pastry chef's apprenticeship and continued throughout his or her career.

Do not forget:

1. Practice makes perfect. The more often the pastry chef uses the paper cone for decoratir.g cakes and pastries, the more quickly the desired result will be achieved.

2. Mastery of paper cone decoration not only requires considerable practice and dexterity, but the pastry chef needs to be familiar with a wide range of designs and writing styles to enhance his or her technique.

In order to master decorating with the paper cone, certain designs need to be closely studied and practiced. Not only is it important to master the shape and style of a particular design, but it is also necessary to be able to execute this design in different sizes, depending on the pastry being decorated.

To become familiar with different designs and writing styles, the beginning pastry chef should practice writing them with a pencil before actually executing them with the paper cone. This is a quick and easy method for developing the necessary dexterity and familiarity with different designs and writing styles.

Decorating effectively with a paper cone requires not only mastery of technique, but also the development of good taste and a clear aesthetic sense. It is important for the beginning pastry chef to pay attention to the work of master chefs.

Another good method the beginning pastry chef can use to master the paper cone is to first draw a design on a sheet of paper with a pencil. The design should then be placed under a sheet of transparent plastic or other hard, transparent surface with a fi. This design can then be used as a practice model.

The student simply follows the design with the tip of the paper cone. If the plastic is hard, it can be washed and the technique repeated until the particular design is mastered.

**Tips for Beginners**

- Be careful when making the paper cone (see pages 54 to 55).

- Make sure that the decorating mixture is perfectly smooth and contains no lumps or particles.

- Cut the tip from the paper cone very carefully.

- Do not use too much force when pressing on the cone. This can cause the tip to tear. Avoid touching the tip of the cone to a wet or moist surface, which can wet it and cause it to tear. Never touch the tip of the cone with the mouth.

- Select a stable and well-lit work area when decorating with a paper cone.

- Position yourself firmly, with both feet held somewhat apart. The back should be bent so you are directly over the piece to be decorated.

- Hold the paper cone with one hand. The other arm should serve as a support to help stabilize the hand doing the decoration.

- Hold the elbows away from the body.

- Decide which method you are going to use. Three methods can be used to decorate with a paper cone:

  **a. thread method**
  **b. sliding method**
  **c. applied method**

Each of these methods uses a slightly different technique.

# The three methods for using a paper cone

**a. Thread method (top photo)**
**b. Sliding method (center photo)**
**c. Applied method (bottom photo)**

# Making a paper cone

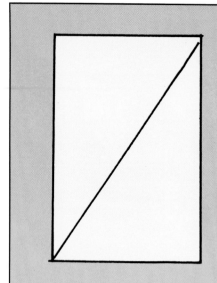

A. Rectangle of parchment paper

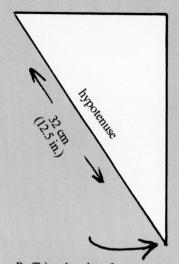

B. Triangle taken from the rectangle (two cones can be made from one rectangle)

32 cm (12.5 in.)

hypotenuse

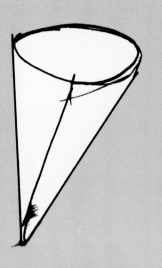

C. The edge of the paper on the outside of the cone is called the holder

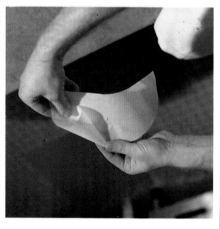

## Making the Cone

Several methods can be used to make a paper cone, all of which give similar results. Regardless of which method is used, the cone should be constructed very carefully.

The paper cone is much like a fountain pen in that the condition of the tip will influence the final outcome of the writing. Do not try to use a badly made cone. If the cone comes out poorly, start over.

The paper used for paper cones should be firm and strong yet flexible. It should be resistant to moisture. Special parchment paper is available for this purpose.

The paper cone is prepared from a triangle of parchment paper which in turn is cut from a rectangle (see diagram above).

The hypotenuse of the triangle should measure 32 cm (12.5 in.) and the base about 16 cm (6.5 in.).

Fold the triangle in on itself with the fold near the center of the hypotenuse directly across from the right angle.

Pinch the hypotenuse of the triangle with the thumb and forefinger in the spot where the fold forms a point. Hold the right angle upward.

Wrap the base of the triangle (pointing downward) around in the other direction. Make sure that it wraps firmly around the cone and that the tip is well formed.

Once the cone has been completely rolled, a flap of paper should remain over the top edge. Fold this over the inside of the cone. Make sure that it is folded tightly. If it comes undone, the cone will unfold.

Check the tip of the cone by aiming it at a light and looking through it. The tip should be completely closed.

The tip of the cone should be cut evenly and quickly with a scissors. Support the scissors with a finger to stabilize them.

Lay the tip of the cone against the bottom blade of the scissors. The cone should form a 90-degree angle with the scissors, so that the end of the tip is perpendicular to the direction of the cone.

Be very careful to not cut too much off the tip: 1 mm (1/20 in.)—about the thickness of a dime—is usually the best amount to cut. Remember, if the tip is too small, it can always be cut a second time, but if it is too large, it will be necessary to start over.

Pipe out a bit of filling to verify that the tip is correctly cut.

### Filling the Paper Cone

Be sure that the filling has the right consistency, the right color, and is free of lumps before filling the cone.

It is best to make the paper cone just before it is filled and to use it as soon as possible.

Do not overfill it, or it will be difficult to close. If the cone contains too much filling, too much pressure will have to be applied to it, which will tire the hand and cause it to tremble.

### Closing the Cone (see diagram)

Make sure the holder (the edge of paper running along the length the cone) is held in the center.

Fold over the top of the cone by folding the paper over itself in 1–cm (3/8–in.) sections. Make sure that the edge of the paper (the holder) is running along the outside of the folds.

This causes the paper to pull up along the cone and helps hold the tip firm and in place.

When the top has been folded inward, fold in the sides and fold the top over the side folds. The cone should be compact and tightly sealed so that none of the filling can escape.

### Cutting the Tip

This is a delicate operation. If the tip of the cone is badly cut, it will be necessary to start over and make another cone.

The paper cone can be cut in several ways, depending on which method is going to be used for the decoration.

The most frequently used of the methods mentioned above is the thread method, which is used for writing, decorative borders, and arabesques.

### Holding the Paper Cone

The paper cone is held between three fingers near the back, away from the tip.

The cone should be held between the index finger and the middle finger, with the thumb pressing against the back, much like holding a syringe. It is the thumb that applies pressure and regulates the flow of the decorating mixture.

At times the index finger and middle finger of the other hand may be used to guide the tip of the cone in especially delicate situations.

# The three methods of decorating with a paper cone

## A. Thread Method

This method is the most frequently used.

### Uses

The thread method is used to decorate the surfaces of cakes and pastries that have soft or semiliquid icings, so that the paper cone cannot touch the surfaces. The method should be used for pastries and cakes coated with:

- butter cream
- soft fondant
- fruit-preserve-based glazes

The thread method is used to make elaborate lettering, arabesques, and borders.

### Holding the Paper Cone

a. Hold the cone between the index finger, middle finger, and thumb.
b. Pressure should be applied with the thumb only, which should be held over the back of the cone.
c. The other hand can be used to help guide the cone over the surface being decorated.

*Important:* The tip of the cone should be very fine.

### Positioning the Cone

Hold the cone directly over the surface of the pastry. It should be perfectly vertical.

The tip of the cone should be held from 3 to 5 cm (1 to 2 in.) over the top of the pastry being decorated. The distance depends to some degree on the type of filling being used—royal icing, cocoa-based decorating mixture, butter cream—and also on the style of decoration. Never stop while executing a design, as this will interfere with its smooth, flowing appearance.

### Starting to Decorate

Position the tip of the cone over the part of the pastry where the decoration is to begin.

Lift the cone above this point while pressing gently but regularly on the back of the cone with the thumb. It requires some skill to ensure that an even, steady flowing thread of mixture is produced.

### Stopping the Decoration

When arriving at the end of a design or motif, slowly reduce the pressure applied to the cone with the thumb and bring the tip down to the surface of the pastry.

*Note:* It is possible to use this method to double and reinforce an already drawn line or design. When doing this, hold the tip of the cone a few millimeters (1/16 to 1/4 in.) from the surface of the pastry being decorated.

## B. Sliding Method

A very firmly constructed cone is required for this technique. It is best to use a piece of paper large enough for the cone to have three layers of paper forming its walls. The tip of the cone should be very solid.

The sliding method is quick and gives good results, but it requires familiarity with the cone and considerable dexterity. The technique also has the advantage of allowing the pastry chef to graduate the thickness of lines.

### Uses

The method can be used on any horizontal surface but only on hard coatings and icings such as:

- crusty fondant
- firm marzipan
- nougatine
- couverture chocolate

The sliding method can be used to make borders, fancy letters, and arabesques, as well as assorted motifs and designs.

*Important:* The tip of the cone should be slightly larger for the sliding method than for the thread method. The sliding method is the method most often used for extremely fancy designs.

### Holding the Cone

The technique is the same as for the thread method.

### Positioning the Cone

Hold the cone at a 30-degree angle over the cake or pastry being decorated.

The tip of the cone should barely brush the surface of the cake or pastry.

When using this method, it is imperative to know exactly how the design is to be executed, because it is important to work quickly.

Stopping the decoration is easy. Simply stop applying pressure with the thumb.

# C. Applied Method

### Uses

The applied method can be used on both horizontal and vertical surfaces. It can be used on either soft semiliquid icings and coatings or on crusty, hard coatings.

This method is most often used to reinforce already existing borders, lettering, and arabesques.

Unlike the other two methods, the pastry chef can lean on the table or work surface.

### Holding the Cone

The technique is the same as for the other two methods.

### Positioning the Cone

Position depends on the surface being decorated:

- On a soft surface, the tip of the cone should lightly brush against the top of the pastry being decorated.

- On a hard or crusty surface, the tip of the cone can be gently pressed against the pastry or cake.

This method can also be used to add final touches to already existing designs.

### Tips for Using the Cone

If a particle gets stuck in the tip of the cone, squeeze the cone tip between the thumb and index finger so as to apply pressure from inside the tip. This should force out the particle.

If the decorating mixture forms a helix or spiral shape as it comes out of the tip, cut the tip back slightly.

Do not ever crush the tip of the cone.

Avoid pressing the tip of the cone too firmly against the surface being decorated.

Never touch the tip of the cone to the mouth. Not only is this unsanitary, but it will soften the tip of the cone and make it unusable.

# Examples of cakes decorated

# with a paper cone

# Examples of miniature cakes decorated

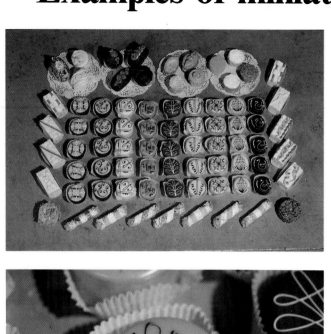

# with a pastry bag and paper cone

# Decorating with a brush

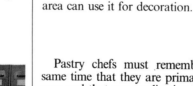

Even though painting is rarely used to decorate pastry, it offers interesting possibilities and can be used to give special shading and nuances.

Pastry chefs must remember at the same time that they are primarily craftsmen and that any application in the field of decoration should be thought of as a craft rather than fine art.

The commercial practicalities of the pastry chef's craft necessarily limit the extent to which even the talented chef can exercise his or her skill as a painter.

Even though the final decoration of pastries is extremely important, it is still secondary to the taste and intrinsic quality of the pastry itself.

Elaborate painting takes many hours of work and is rarely practical in a commercial situation.

Obviously not every pastry chef is expected to master painting techniques, but those who have an ability in this area can use it for decoration.

Decorating pastry with a brush can be divided into four categories:

### 1. Shading

The techniques of shading are relatively easy to master. Sometimes a sponge is used for larger surfaces.

### 2. Painting with Cocoa Powder

This is an inexpensive and versatile technique.

### 3. Painting with Food Coloring

This is the most difficult of the painting techniques. The nuances of color must be controlled in the same way as watercolors.

### 4. Painting Backgrounds

Sometimes three-dimensional decoration is painted with food coloring or cocoa powder. This technique is relatively easy to execute.

# Preparing surfaces for painting

Whatever the technique used for painting, a firm surface, or *substrate,* must be prepared to function as the base. The painting substrate is usually composed of one of three materials:

1. Pastillage

2. Marzipan

3. Chocolate

## 1. Painting on Pastillage

The pastillage should be rolled out into thin sheets and cut into the desired shapes before being slowly dried.

It is important that the drying take place slowly to prevent the edges of the pastillage from curling.

Before beginning to paint on pastillage, lightly scrape its surface with the blade of a knife to make sure that it is perfectly smooth. Be sure to place the sheet of pastillage on several layers of kitchen towels to prevent it from breaking.

If the surface of the pastillage is to be painted with food coloring, the pastillage should first be glazed in the oven with a coating of gelatin dissolved in water.

This glazing creates an impermeable coating on the surface of the pastillage. Otherwise, the surface acts like a blotter and may cause the colors to bleed and run into each other.

## 2. Painting on Marzipan

It is best to roll out sheets of marzipan 24 to 48 hours in advance so that a light crust forms on the surfaces. The crust will prevent the food colorings from being too readily absorbed into the marzipan.

## 3. Painting on Chocolate

When painting on a chocolate substrate, make sure that it is shiny and perfectly smooth. In general, these substrates are made of white chocolate. It is best to prepare chocolate substrates for painting shortly before they are to be used. Otherwise the chocolate tends to soften and lose its sheen.

# Painting and shading with cocoa

Cocoa powder can be added to a small amount of oil or water and used to shade and give a three-dimensional effect to designs, writing, and motifs. The technique is also used to create shadows and to tint the background of a drawing to give the appearance of old parchment. The cocoa mixture can be applied with a small brush, a sponge, or the tip of the finger.

Whichever method is used, the technique offers the pastry chef the opportunity to control and graduate the depth of color used for the shading. The depth of color is controlled by applying fine layers of cocoa mixture.

## Painting with Cocoa

Because cocoa powder is inexpensive, it provides an opportunity for the beginning pastry chef to develop dexterity and painting skill before moving on to more expensive multiple colors.

## Substrates

The same types of substrates can be used as when painting with food coloring: pastillage, chocolate, and marzipan.

## Choosing the Subject

It is best to start painting simpler subjects such as landscapes, in which a certain amount of variation in the principal lines is acceptable. When first painting these subjects, it is best to work from a photograph. Soon it will be possible to execute some of these drawings from memory as they become part of the pastry chef's repertoire. After a certain amount of skill with the brush has been developed, the beginning chef should move on to other, more difficult subjects, such as birds and small animals.

The most difficult paintings to execute are portraits, where the slightest variation will alter the final effect.

## Technique for Painting with Cocoa

Whatever the subject, it is best to start the painting by first preparing a kind of transfer sheet with parchment paper.

### Preparing the Transfer Sheet

The subject is traced with a pencil from a photograph onto a piece of stiff, transparent parchment paper. The parchment paper is then turned over, and the other side is brushed with cocoa that has been worked with a little water.

The side with the brushed cocoa is then allowed to dry so that a thin film of dried cocoa powder remains. Once the cocoa has dried, the parchment paper is turned over on the substrate. The pencil lines are again retraced so that the cocoa is transferred to the substrate in the same way as if this were carbon paper. Once this outline has been transferred to the substrate, the painting only has to be shaded and filled in with additional decoration.

To finish the painting, it is best to have available an array of different-sized brushes for shading and filling in details.

*Tips for the Beginner*

Be sure to work in a well-lit area, preferably with natural light.

Prepare the equipment:

● small brushes

● small plate with a tablespoon of cocoa powder

● a glass containing a small amount of oil or water (oil gives a brighter color but takes longer to dry and is harder to work with).

● a small paring knife with a sharp tip to scrape away mistakes

● a clean kitchen towel or rag to clean the brushes

● a photograph or model to work from

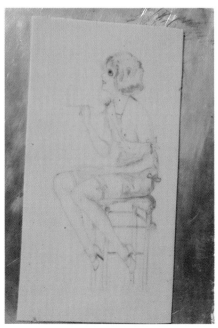

## Filling in the Outline

Place the cocoa powder in the center of a small plate. With a moist brush, push a small amount of the cocoa away from the center of the plate. Work the cocoa powder with a bit of water at the edge of the plate.

Work the cocoa until it has the desired depth of color.

Before beginning the actual painting, it is advisable to test the color of the cocoa mixture by brushing some of it onto the same material used as the substrate (for example, onto a piece of pastillage).

This is the best way to judge its color depth, which can then be adjusted accordingly. If no additional substrate material is available, test the mixture on a piece of white cardboard.

It is better to use a light-colored cocoa mixture than a mixture that is too dark. If the mixture is light, the shading can be reinforced by painting additional coats. If, on the other hand, the mixture is too dark, the process is irreversible. One charming aspect of painting with cocoa is that the paintings resemble old-fashioned sepia photographs.

## Shading

Hold the wet brush at a 45-degree angle against the substrate. Paint the darker sections of the painting first and gradually work out to the lighter shades. Go over the darker shades several times until they have the right tone. Use a light touch.

The shading of a section of the painting can also be finished by smoothing it over with the finger. This method is sometimes easier to control than working with a brush.

If a mistake is made, let the cocoa dry completely and then scrape off the section with the tip of a paring knife.

*Note:* Some pastry chefs prefer to start the outline of the painting by using a paper cone (sliding method). This technique is quicker and is used for commercial preparations.

Complete the painting first, before decorating the rim or frame of a painting. Otherwise the frame can interfere with the painting and may get broken in the process.

# Mixing colors

### Using Food Coloring

A wide range of food colorings are now available to the pastry chef. The chemicals used in their preparation are closely controlled by the government.

In the United States, food coloring is usually sold in concentrated liquid form. In France, it is usually sold as powders.

### Preparing Powdered Food Coloring

If using powdered food coloring, it is first necessary to convert it to liquid form. Take a teaspoon of the powdered coloring and place it into a saucepan with 150 ml (5 fl. oz.) of water. Gently heat the saucepan until the powder dissolves. Do not let the mixture come to a boil, or the coloring may coagulate.

Once the mixture has cooled, add 100 ml (3.5 fl. oz.) of strong fruit brandy (such as Kirsch) to preserve it. Strain the coloring through a coffee filter and keep in a tightly sealed bottle.

Today food coloring is available in so many colors that it is rarely necessary to create secondary and tertiary colors by blending two separate colors, which can be a tricky process.

Food coloring is often used in pastry making, but the pastry chef should remember not to abuse it and certainly not to use too many colors in the same preparation.

For example, when covering a cake with marzipan, pale pink is far more appealing than white. Red, however, is too bright and would be unappetizing. Bright red, on the other hand, is perfectly appropriate for coloring roses and other flowers.

### Intensity of Color

It is of course possible to obtain a wide range of color intensities with a single color (see photo above).

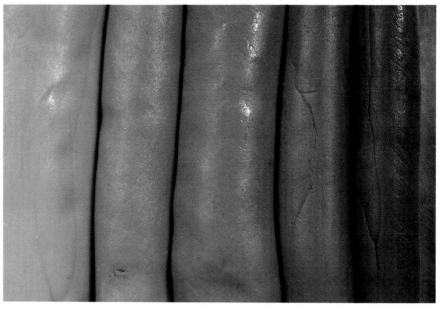

### Combining Colors

Food coloring can be combined in the same way as any paint to form secondary and tertiary colors.

Remember that a secondary color is based on a mixture of two primary colors. Various tones can be obtained by combining these primary colors in unequal amounts.

For example, when a small amount of red food coloring is added to a relatively large amount of yellow coloring, yellow-orange is obtained.

By starting with the three primary colors, blue, red, and yellow, it is possible to produce the whole spectrum of colors, as can be seen below on the color wheel.

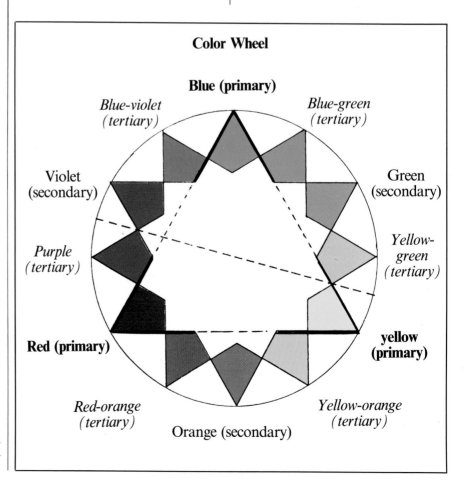

**Color Wheel**

Blue (primary)
*Blue-violet (tertiary)*
*Blue-green (tertiary)*
Violet (secondary)
Green (secondary)
*Purple (tertiary)*
*Yellow-green (tertiary)*
**Red (primary)**
**yellow (primary)**
*Red-orange (tertiary)*
*Yellow-orange (tertiary)*
Orange (secondary)

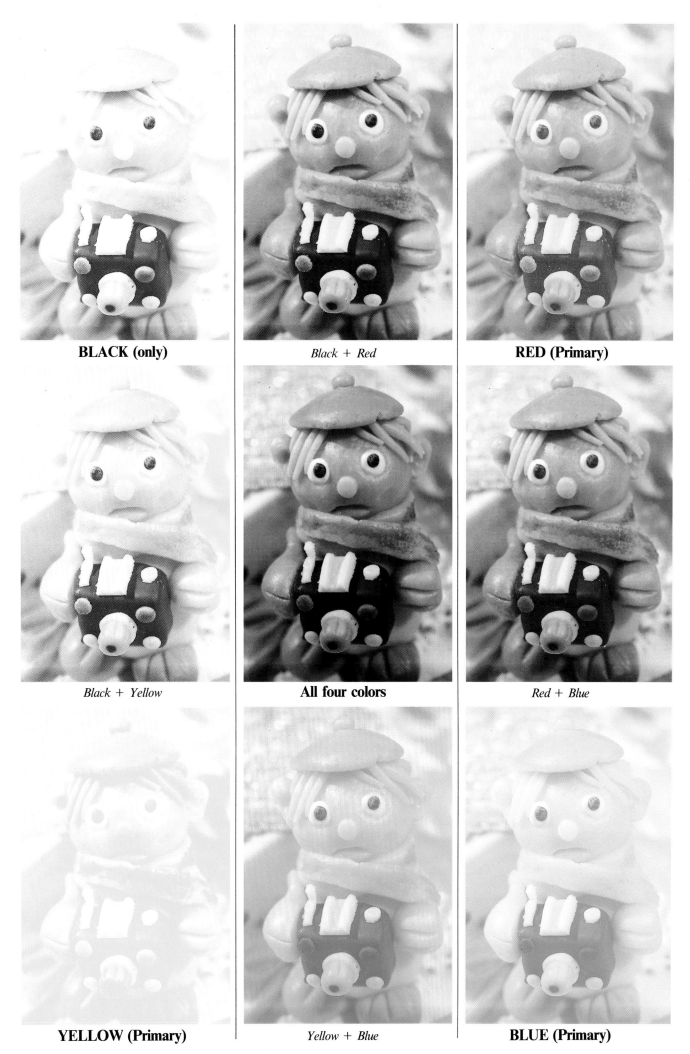

**BLACK (only)**

*Black + Red*

**RED (Primary)**

*Black + Yellow*

**All four colors**

*Red + Blue*

**YELLOW (Primary)**

*Yellow + Blue*

**BLUE (Primary)**

63

# Painting with food coloring

**Painting with food coloring is the most difficult and sophisticated technique used by the pastry chef. It is rarely used because it is impractical in commercial establishments. The technique, however, allows the pastry chef to use his or her artistry for galas and special occasions.**

Remember that the fundamental rule underlying even the most elaborate decorating techniques is the principle that only edible ingredients should be used.

### Tips for the Beginner

Prepare the substrates for the painting and make a first sketch either by hand or with a transfer sheet.

The work station should be organized in the same way as when painting with cocoa. Painting with food coloring is more difficult than painting with cocoa for obvious reasons. Considerable experience is required to master the technique.

The superimposition of colors is not always predictable and requires an ability to predict the outcome, which can only come with experience.

Portraits are the most difficult because the slightest variation in color or line affects the final result.

### Setting Up the Food Coloring

Put several drops of each type of food coloring in small plates or tartlet molds.

The colors should be well diluted with a clear liquor such as vodka. Remember to have an extra piece of the substrate material available so that the colors can be tested as they are combined.

Beginning pastry chefs tend to use colors that are too intense. Remember that the colors become brighter as they dry. It is best to use very pale colors, which can always be reinforced with additional coats.

One of the advantages of the alcohol-based food coloring solutions is that they dry very quickly. Because of this, it is easy to make adjustments in the depth of color by adding additional coats if necessary.

When painting with food coloring, it is imperative that the substrate be glazed before painting. Otherwise the colors tend to bleed and run into one another.

When using colors, it is difficult to scrape off a section if a mistake has been made, as once the glaze is removed from a section of the support, the food coloring tends to penetrate into the porous base and form unsightly rings.

The subject matter used for painting with food coloring is the same as for painting with cocoa.

# Spraying color

In addition to painting with a brush, several other methods can be used to apply color to the surfaces of pastries.

The methods include:

1. Sprinkling with a brush

2. Spraying with an atomizer

3. Using an airbrush

## 1. Sprinkling with a Brush

This very simple method enables the pastry chef to sprinkle the surface of certain decorations with droplets of coloring. The technique is used primarily for meringue mushrooms and certain flowers.

Use a small brush with fairly rigid fibers. A toothbrush or fingernail brush works well. Dip the ends of the brush fibers in the liquid coloring. Hold the brush sideways over the piece to be colored. Lightly scrape the brush fibers with the back of a paring knife to spatter the coloring in a fine mist.

The size of the droplets can be controlled by holding the brush varying distances from the surface being decorated.

## 2. Spraying with an Atomizer

The atomizer is a miniature tube used to disperse colorings in a fine mist.

The food coloring must be completely liquid and free of extraneous particles.

Dip the end of the metal tube into the food coloring. Blow into one end of the tube, aiming it so the mist lands on the surface being decorated.

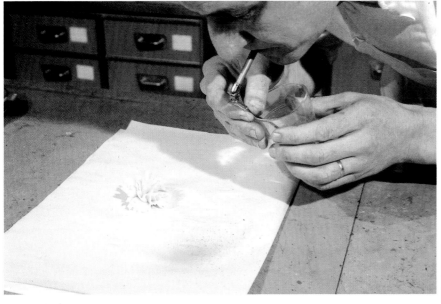

*Note*

Coloring of the surface area can be controlled by thinning the food coloring and by pulling away from the surface being decorated.

The farther away the spray source is, the greater the surface area that will be covered.

It is sometimes necessary to protect the areas surrounding the section being decorated by masking them with pieces of paper or cardboard.

Even though the mist produced by an atomizer is difficult to control, it can still be used to paint shadows behind flowers and other decorations.

The intensity of color produced by the atomizer can be controlled by altering its angle in relation to the surface being decorated.

## 3. Using an Airbrush

The use of the airbrush is a recent innovation in professional pastry making.

Although the equipment used is somewhat expensive, the technique is used more and more frequently by pastry chefs.

The airbrush is a miniature gun that atomizes paint or food coloring with compressed air. Relatively little air pressure is required.

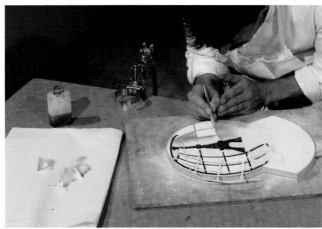

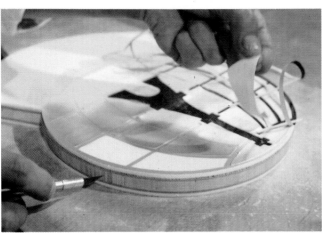

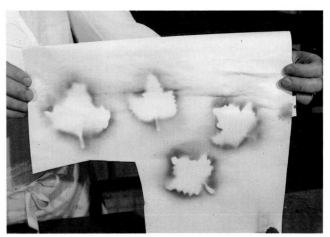

# Examples of coloring

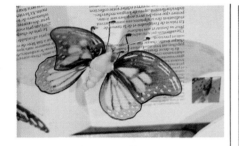

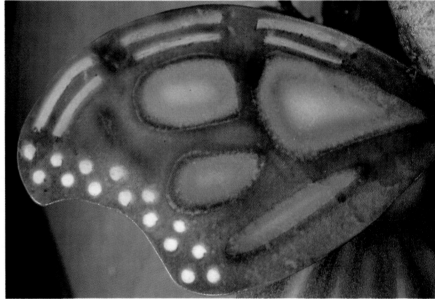

# applied with an airbrush

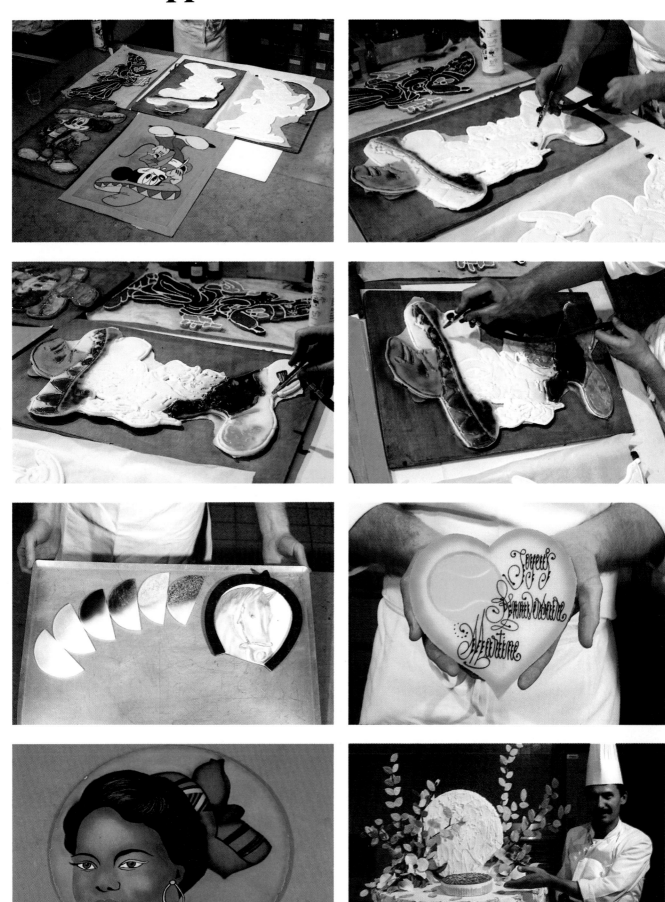

# Relief painting

With this method Italian meringue or royal icing is colored and then applied to a surface with a pastry brush or paper cone.

When using a pastry brush, dip the brush in the diluted food coloring and stir it with a given quantity of Italian meringue. Continue combining coloring and Italian meringue until the desired shade and depth of color is obtained.

When using a paper cone, fill it with either royal icing or Italian meringue.

Dip the tip of the cone in food coloring. The food coloring will work its way up into the cone by capillary action. The paper cone is then used to outline backgrounds and shadings in different colors. The tip of the cone should be dipped into the food coloring as often as necessary while applying either the colored meringue or royal icing to the surface of the painting.

When colored meringue or royal icing is applied to the surface of a painting, it remains raised on the surface and makes it three dimensional. It does not produce a smooth surface in the same way as painting with cocoa or food coloring. It is because of this three-dimensional effect that these ingredients are used for painting in relief.

Relief painting does not allow the pastry chef the same freedom as painting with cocoa or food coloring does.

It can, however, be used for rapid painting of simpler designs and motifs (flowers, landscapes, seascapes, and birds) on the surfaces of cakes.

Relief paintings are usually applied to cakes that are covered with a sheet of marzipan. Relief painting can also be used on the surfaces of prepared bases that are later placed on the tops of cakes.

Practice painting one or two simple designs that can be easily mastered.

Eventually, depending on skill, the pastry chef should be able to develop a repertoire of designs or motifs that can be quickly executed from memory.

**(continued on next page)**

# Scratched surface decoration

This method consists of scratching the surface of a substrate that has been covered with a thin film of cocoa. In this way the film of cocoa forms the background to the decoration, which is actually the surface of the substrate showing through.

**Procedure**

Use solid substrates of pastillage, marzipan, or white chocolate. Spread either part or all of the surface of the substrate with cocoa decorating mixture, using either a pastry brush or the tip of the finger. Let the cocoa mixture dry before beginning the scratching.

Use either the tip of a sharp paring knife or a piece of wood that has been sharpened like a pencil without lead. Scratch the surface of the cocoa-covered substrate to form the design.

This method can be combined with other decorating techniques using a paper cone.

---

**(relief painting, continued)**

The colored meringue or royal icing can be applied to a firm substrate made of either marzipan or pastillage. It is also possible to relief-paint on a smooth surface of Italian meringue, Swiss meringue, or royal icing.

Several techniques can be used to execute certain design elements quickly. To paint a sky, for example, roughly spread the surface of the cake with Italian meringue.

Put a small amount of blue food coloring on the tip of the finger and brush it over the Italian meringue so that the surface is spread unevenly with the blue color.

This gives the effect of a natural-looking cloudy sky. The same method can be used to paint bodies of water.

It is also possible to paint with colored meringues and a knife. The technique is similar to oil painting.

Relief painting can also be done with uncolored ingredients. The surface is then allowed to harden, and the relief is painted with food coloring, using a pastry brush.

# Chapter 2
# Decorative borders and lettering

~~~~~~~~~~~~~~~

Even though the final decoration of cakes and pastries is largely a question of personal style, certain writing techniques and designs should be mastered by every pastry chef.

The simplest designs and writing styles are often the most appealing. The following pages contain examples of the most frequently used basic design styles and lettering methods.

Because of space limitations, the pictures that follow show the size of the lettering and designs reduced by four. To reproduce the actual size, enlarge the designs four times.

# Decorative borders

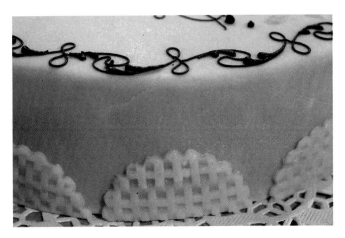

## Definition

Grouped under the heading decorative borders are a wide range of designs that can be used around the sides and top edges of cakes.

Designs placed around the edges of cakes not only serve a decorative role, but can also be used to indicate the flavor of the cake to the consumer.

It is important that border designs be mastered with a pencil and paper before the beginning pastry chef moves on to applying them to a finished cake with a paper cone.

Some of the designs must be repeated many times before the pastry chef will feel confident enough to apply them to a finished cake.

When practicing these designs with the paper cone, remember to keep the fingers relaxed.

If the hand and fingers are held too tightly around the cone, the spontaneous and free-flowing look of the design may be lost.

*Below, the principal border designs have been divided into five main families:*

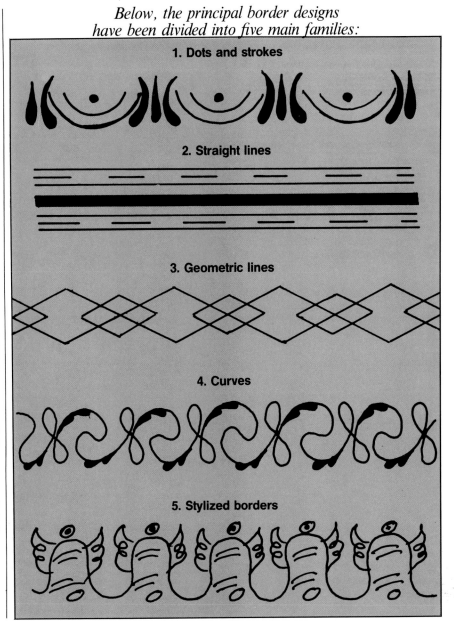

1. Dots and strokes

2. Straight lines

3. Geometric lines

4. Curves

5. Stylized borders

## Dots and Strokes

These are the simplest decorations to learn. When first using the paper cone for decorating cakes, these designs should be practiced first.

## Straight-line Borders

These are applied using the thread method with a paper cone. They are characterized by their direction—vertical, horizontal, or diagonal—as well as by their relationship to each other—parallel, perpendicular, or intersecting at other angles. They can be applied in different thicknesses. Thick layers can be used to give relief to the surface of a cake or pastry.

These designs can be applied directly to the surface of a cake, or they can be applied to a sheet of stiff plastic, allowed to dry, gently lifted off the plastic, and then put on cakes as needed.

## Geometric-line Borders

These are applied using the thread method with a paper cone. A wide variety of designs and decorations can be applied using this method.

Geometric-line borders are quite difficult to execute and require considerable experience with a paper cone.

## Curved Borders

Curved borders are the most frequently used by the professional pastry chef because they offer an almost limitless range of possibilities.

Most curved decorations for borders are prepared using the thread method with a paper cone. At times, the sliding method is also used. The two techniques can be combined and used on the same cake.

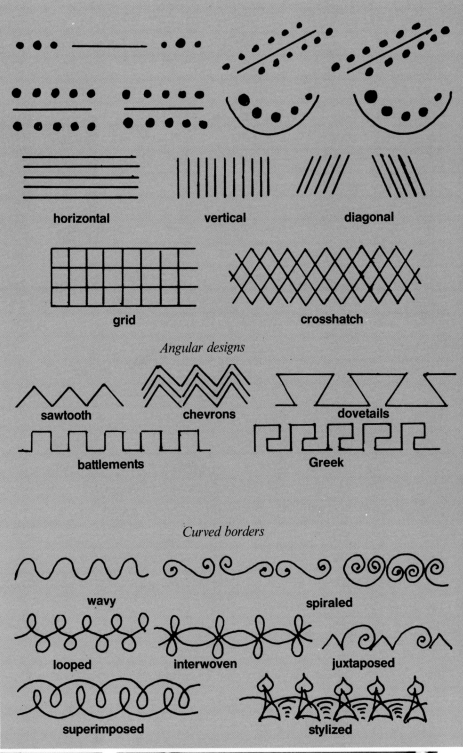

**horizontal**    **vertical**    **diagonal**

**grid**    **crosshatch**

*Angular designs*

**sawtooth**    **chevrons**    **dovetails**

**battlements**    **Greek**

*Curved borders*

**wavy**    **spiraled**

**looped**    **interwoven**    **juxtaposed**

**superimposed**    **stylized**

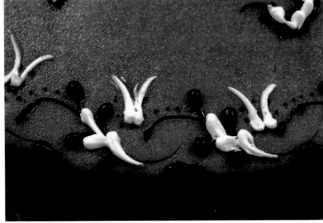

# Examples of borders

## Tips on Applying Decorative Borders

Try to coordinate the style of the border with any writing that has been applied to the center of the cake. Ornate curved writing should have a similar border. Bolder, more modern lettering should have a more linear border.

Avoid applying too large a border to the edge of a cake. This can distract the eye from the cake's decoration and make it seem smaller than it actually is. Border designs should always be light and delicate and should be applied as close to the top edge of the cake as possible. It is even advantageous to extend the border down the sides of the cake, as this makes the cake appear thicker.

In most cases, decorative borders should be applied with a very fine tip.

## Dots and strokes

## Geometric-line borders (1)

## Geometric-line borders (2)

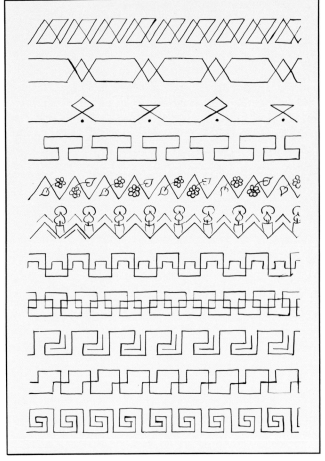

# Examples of borders

## Wavy borders (1)

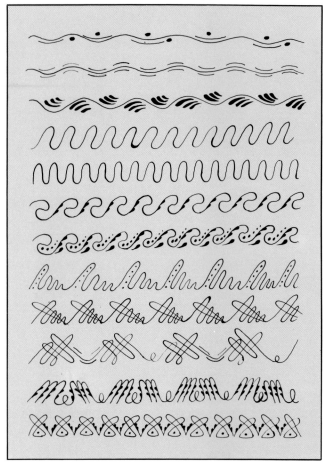

## Wavy borders (2)

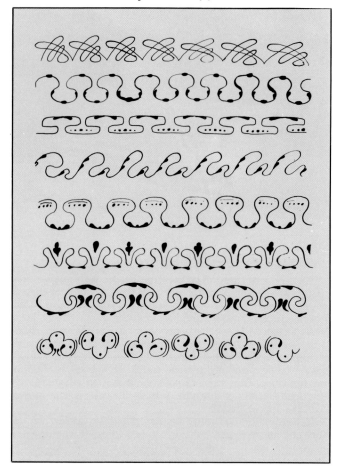

## S-shaped borders (1)

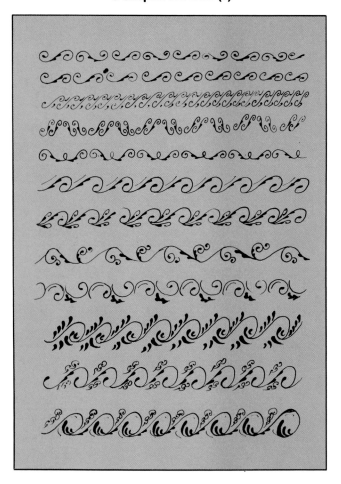

## S-shaped borders (2)

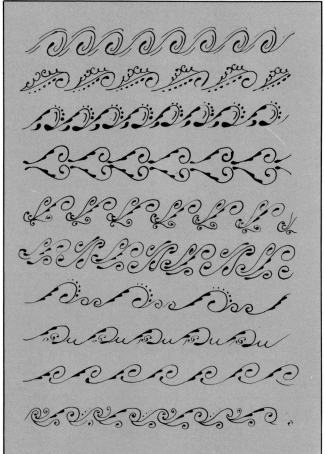

**Looped borders (1)**

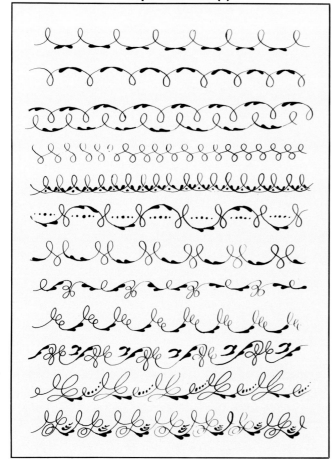

**Looped borders (3)**

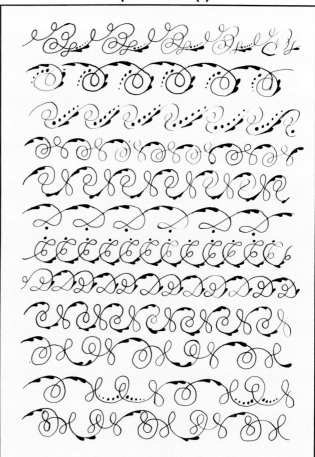

**Looped borders (2)**

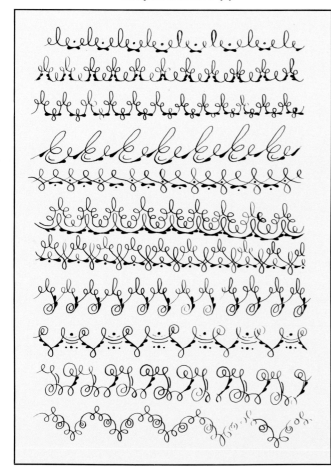

**Looped borders (4)**

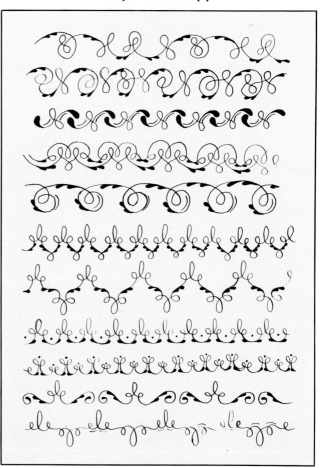

# Examples of borders

### Spiral borders

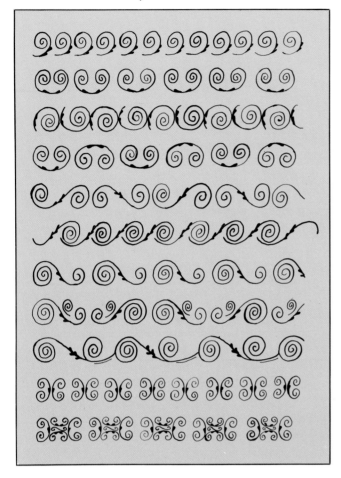

### Interwoven borders (1)

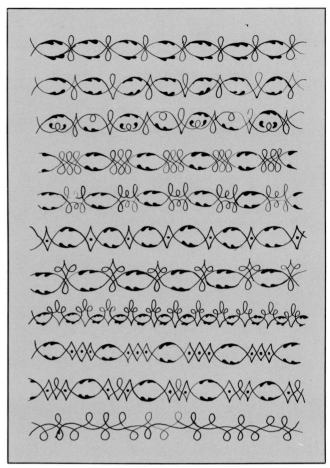

### Interwoven borders (2)

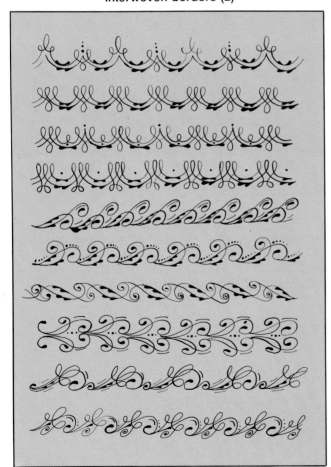

### Interwoven borders (3)

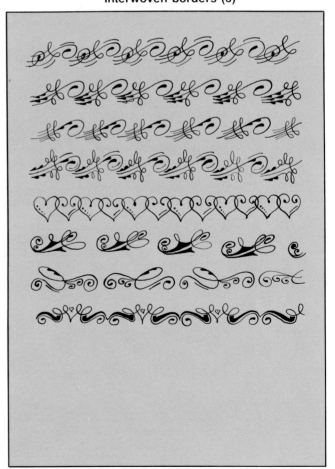

## Stylized borders (1)

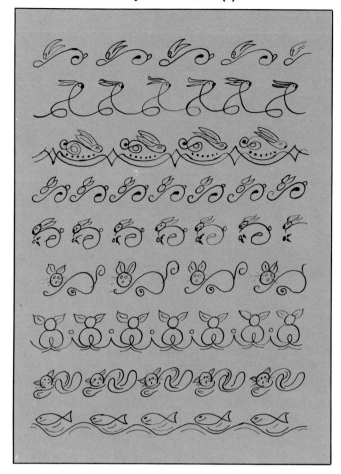

## Stylized borders (2)

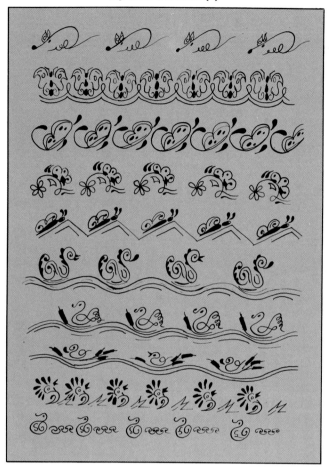

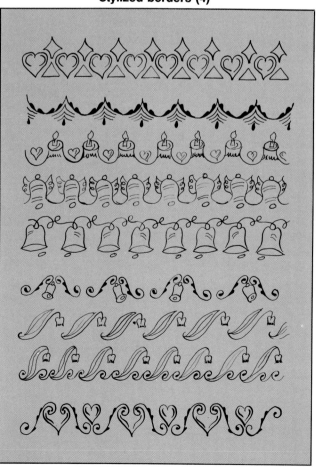

79

# Examples of borders

**Juxtaposed borders (1)**

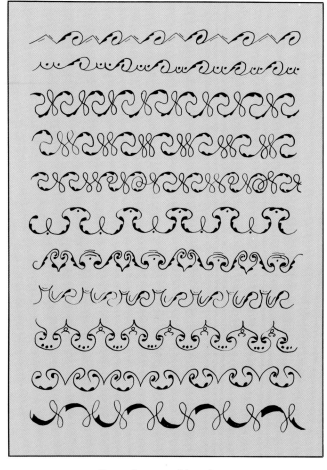

**Juxtaposed borders (2)**

**Superimposed borders**

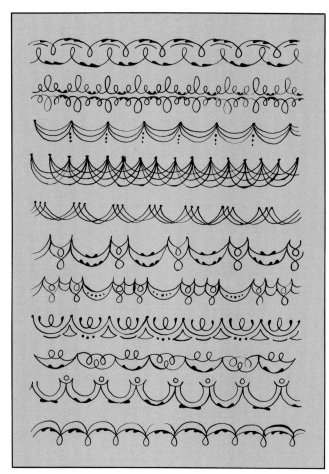

# Writing and lettering styles

*Decoration is one of the most important aspects of the pastry chef's art and perhaps the most difficult to master. Once the pastry chef has mastered the basic lettering and decorating styles, he or she is free to invent new decorations and presentations.*

*If a cake or pastry is poorly decorated, it will fail to tempt the appetite and will go unappreciated, no matter how carefully constructed and flavored. The decoration of a finished dessert should stimulate interest and appetite.*

## Decoration

Cakes and pastries should be decorated according to their composition and final use. Some decorative writing indicates the flavorings used in the construction of the cake.

When a cake is ordered in advance in a restaurant or pastry shop, it is imperative that all necessary details be recorded. For example, for a birthday the following should be noted:

- the sex of the person whose birthday is being celebrated

- his or her age

- the size of the birthday party—a small family gathering or a larger group of friends

The writing style should be appropriate. A small child's birthday cake should have simple lettering such as the child is likely to learn in school, not ornate, stylized lettering, which would be more appropriate for someone older.

This is one reason why the professional pastry chef should master several writing styles.

In this chapter, several highly diverse lettering styles are presented. It is best to practice the writing styles and letters with a paper and pencil before using a paper cone.

## Professional Writing and Drawing

Pastry chefs usually confine their use of decorative lettering and writing to certain standard styles and patterns. Inscriptions, floral motifs, and arabesques are the most common.

Rarely does a pastry chef give vent to his or her full creativity by inventing original designs and motifs. To a degree this is necessitated by the commercial demands of the pastry chef's craft. At the same time, the talented pastry chef should be able to invent new designs and give his or her finished pastries a personal flair.

The ability to reproduce a given design and transfer it to the surface of a finished pastry requires long practice and a keen eye. Many of the designs and writing styles shown in this book can be mastered only after long hours of practice with a paper and pencil.

Once the letters and designs can be written on paper, the beginning pastry chef should practice applying them to a smooth surface with a paper cone.

All this is required before the design can be applied to a finished pastry.

Decorative lettering also has a valid commercial use—reminding the public of upcoming holidays and special occasions. What better reminder than to walk past a pastry shop a few days before Valentine's Day!

Mastering cake decoration involves the accumulation of a wide variety of individual skills. The experienced pastry chef should be sufficiently familiar with each design and lettering style so that the designs can be drawn lightly and spontaneously.

Eventually the pastry chef will find his or her own personal style and may even have certain signature cakes.

## Lettering Styles

### 1. Block letters

These are the simplest letters and should be practiced before moving on to more complicated styles.

### 2. Double-stroke block letters

### 3. Cursive letters

This is lettering in script.

### 4. Ornate letters

Even though ornate, make sure these letters remain completely legible.

### 5. Modern-style letters

This is highly stylized lettering. Make sure it stays legible.

### 6. Gothic letters

These letters are derived from the style used for medieval manuscripts.

# Examples of lettering styles

## Block letters (1)

Aa Bb Cc Dd Ee
Ff Gg Hh Ii Jj Kk
Ll Mm Nn Oo Pp
Qq Rr Ss Tt Uu
Vv Ww Xx Yy Zz
1 2 3 4 5 6 7 8 9 0
Croissants
CROISSANTS

## Block letters (2)

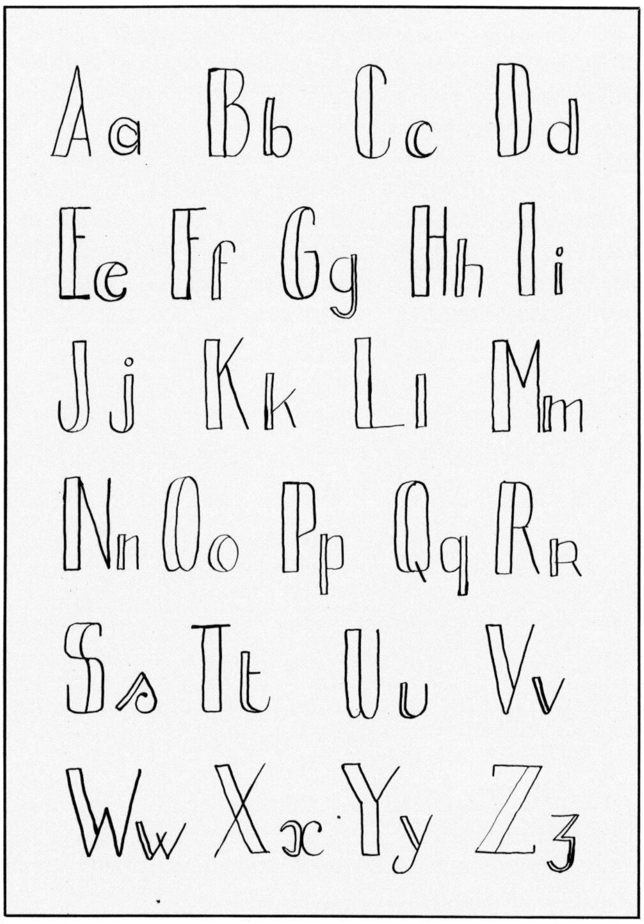

Aa Bb Cc Dd
Ee Ff Gg Hh Ii
Jj Kk Ll Mm
Nn Oo Pp Qq Rr
Ss Tt Uu Vv
Ww Xx Yy Zz

## Double-stroke block letters (3)

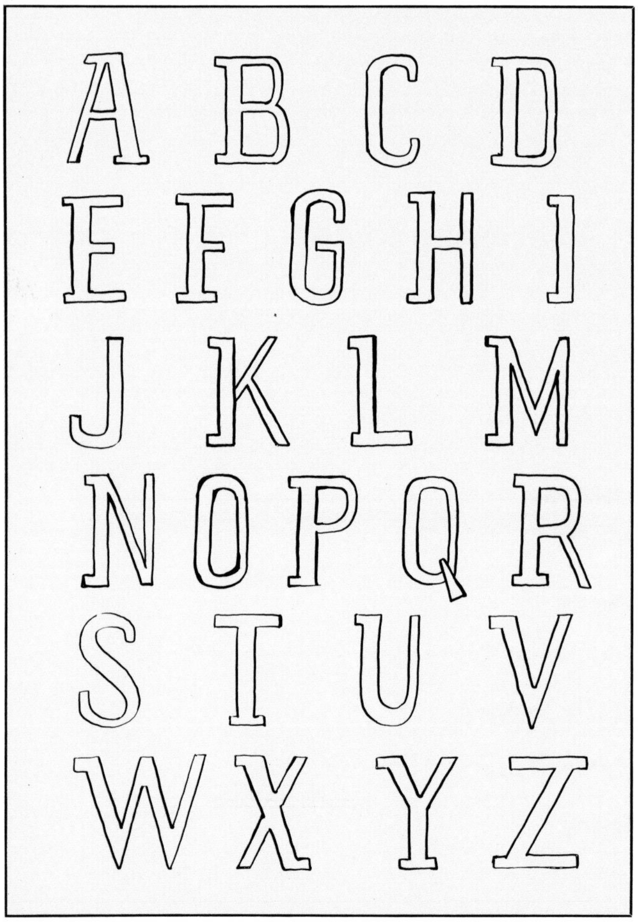

A B C D
E F G H I
J K L M
N O P Q R
S T U V
W X Y Z

## Double-stroke block letters (4)

Aa Bb Cc Dd Ee
Ff Gg Hh Ii Jj Kk
Ll Mm Nn Oo Pp
Qq Rr Ss Tt Uu
Vv Ww Xx Yy Zz
Alexandra
Barbara

## Simple cursive letters

a b b c d d e f f g h
b i j f k k l l m n o
p p q r r s s s t u
v v v w x x y y
z z 1 2 3 4 5 6 7 8 9 0
1 2 3 4 5 6 7 8 9 0

## Cursive letters (1)

## Cursive letters (2)

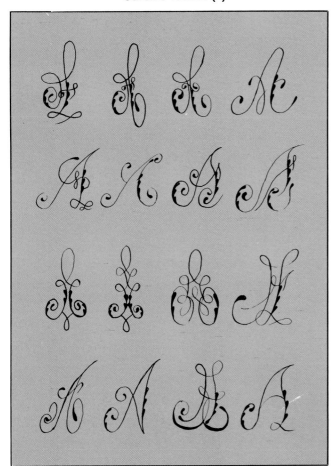

## Cursive letters (3)

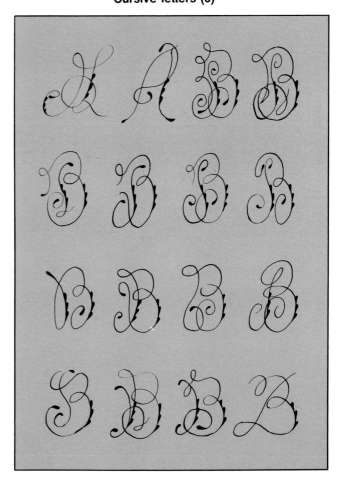

# Examples of lettering styles

### Cursive letters (4)

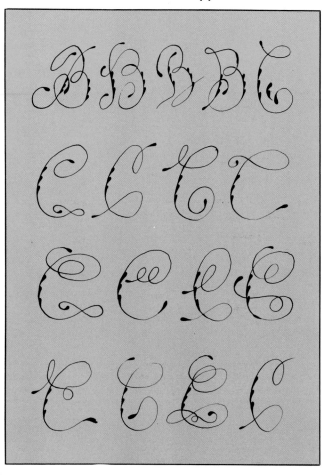

### Cursive letters (5)

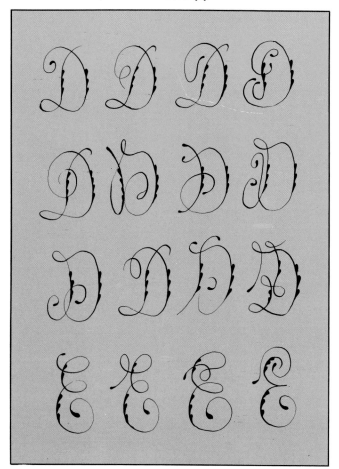

### Cursive letters (6)

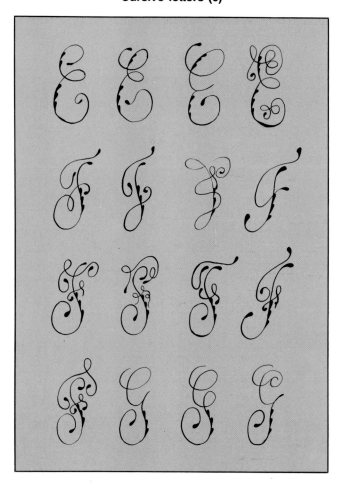

### Cursive letters (7)

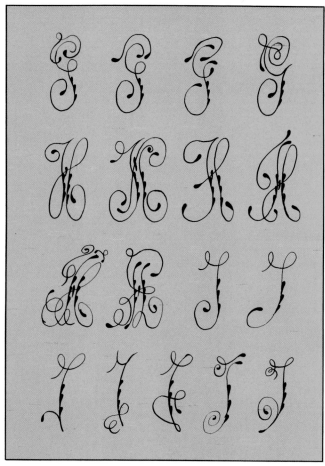

## Cursive letters (8)

## Cursive letters (9)

## Cursive letters (10)

## Cursive letters (11)

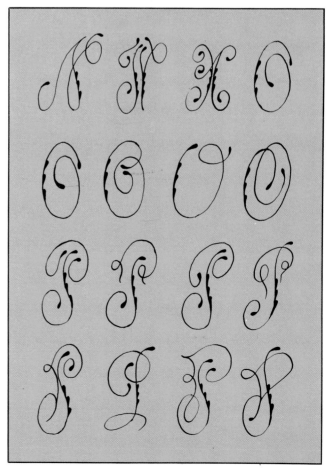

# Examples of lettering styles

**Cursive letters (12)**

**Cursive letters (13)**

**Ornate letters (1)**

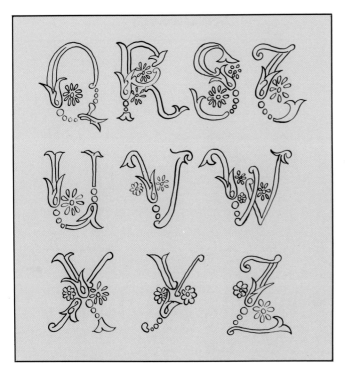

**Ornate letters (2)**

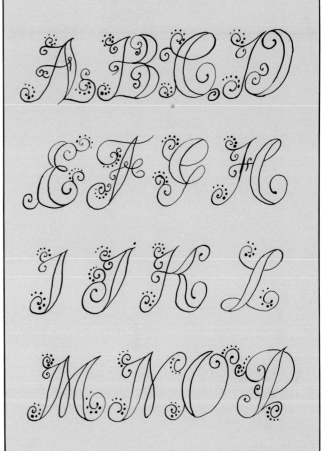

# Examples of lettering styles

**Modern-style letters (1)**

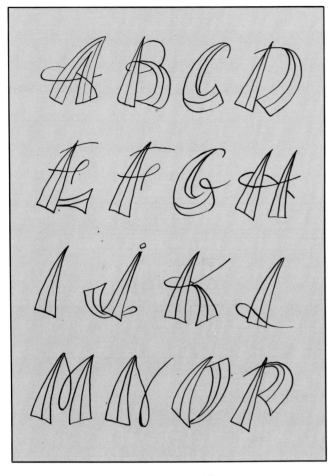

**Modern-style letters (2)**

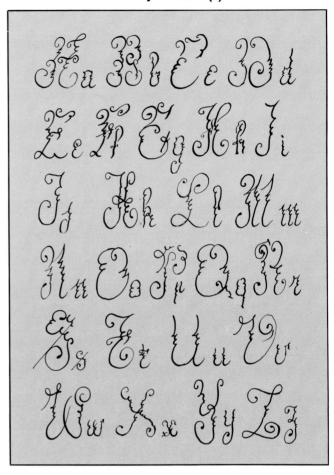

**Gothic letters (1)**

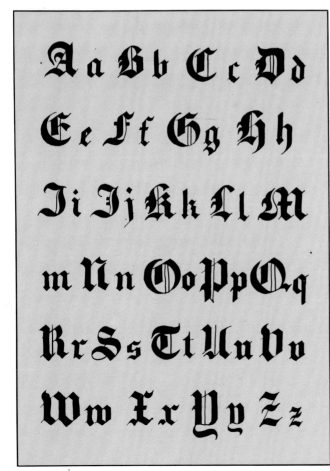

**Gothic letters (2)**

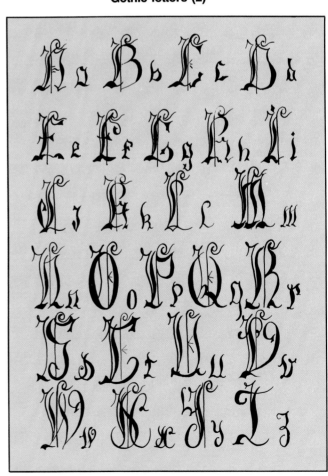

# Inscriptions

When lettering is applied to the surface of a cake or pastry, it has a dual purpose. Not only should it be decorative and give the cake a professional and festive appearance, but it should also convey a message—either the announcement of an event or a simple description of the contents of the cake.

For lettering to be effective, it should be legible and even. Try to calculate as closely as possible the amount of space that will be required for the inscription. It is always a good idea to start a little to the left so as not to run out of room at the end.

The same writing style should be maintained throughout the inscription. This is also true of any decorative border, which should not clash with the type of lettering being used.

Make the best use of capital letters. It is better to exaggerate and make them larger so they contrast with the rest of the lettering and dramatize the design.

Adding decorative swirls and flourishes to fill out lettering (see photo) and arabesques lends a nice touch to the inscription.

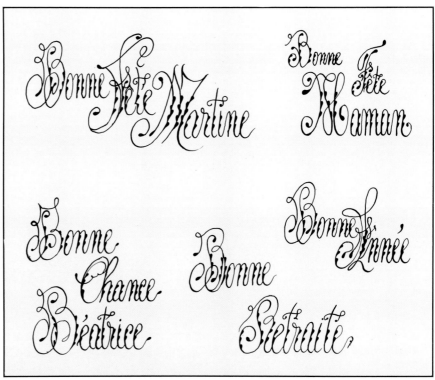

# Examples of lettering styles

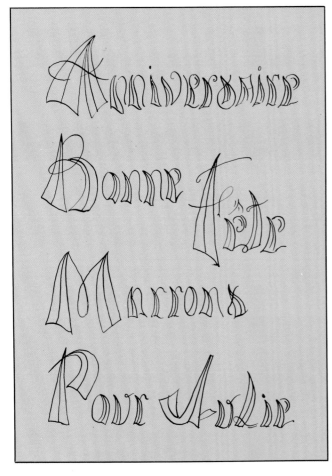

91

# Examples of writing styles

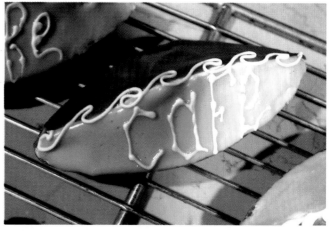

# Assorted drawings and designs

Below are examples of drawings and designs that can be quickly executed with a paper cone using chocolate or royal icing.

Drawings of animals can be especially appropriate for children.

Depending on the type of holiday, different types of animals can be drawn. For example:

● for Christmas: deer and reindeer
● for Easter: ducklings, baby chicks, rabbits

● for birthdays or other special occasions: doves, swans, ducklings, butterflies, fish

Use simple designs that can be drawn rapidly but at the same time produce charming results.

# Arabesques

Arabesques are usually used to augment an already existing design, but for some miniature cakes and petits fours, the decoration may consist of only one or a few arabesques.

### Arabesques (1)

### Arabesques (2)

### Arabesques in squares

### Arabesques in circles

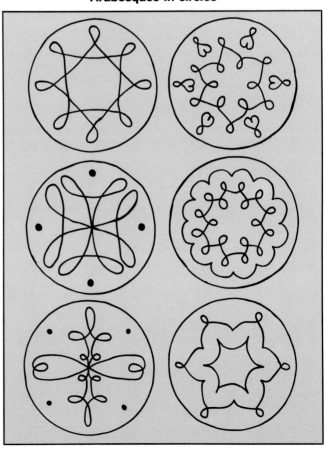

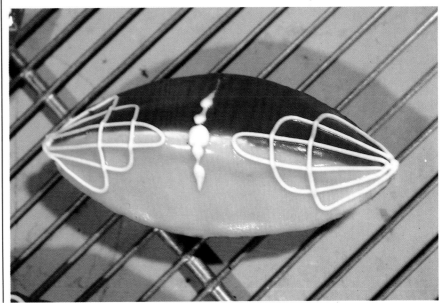

# Flowers and leaves

Leaf and flower designs are usually highly simplified. The pastry chef will often get a better effect by drawing a simplified outline of the subject rather than trying for an interpretation that is too exact or too literal.

These designs are applied with a paper cone using chocolate decorating mixture, royal icing, and sometimes fruit preserves or fondant.

These stylized designs are obtained in two ways: | 1. by sketching the subject as a simple outline | 2. by representing the subject loosely.

# Chapter 3

# Marzipan decorations

Marzipan is extremely versatile because of its malleability and good flavor. It can be shaped in many different ways, making it an extremely useful ingredient for the pastry chef. Working with marzipan requires considerable experience and a good sense of color and proportion.

Because of the importance and versatility of marzipan and its usefulness to the pastry chef, an entire chapter is devoted to its various applications.

This chapter not only describes the best techniques for shaping and coloring marzipan, but also includes a large number of color photos that can serve as examples and models. The examples, techniques, and models have been grouped according to type.

# Various possibilities

### Flowers

*Flowers are usually made to be placed on cakes. The most commonly used are carnations and roses, but some pastry chefs also make other varieties.*

### Leaves

*Leaves are made to accompany flowers and to help them stand out.*

### Fruit

*A large variety of fruit is often prepared by the pastry chef. Its coloring is often tricky and requires considerable experience.*

### Vegetables

*These are relatively simple to shape but, like fruit, require careful coloring.*

### Assorted Subjects

*These can include almost any shape, but the most commonly used special subjects are animals. This is an open category that can allow the pastry chef to invent new shapes and designs.*

### Parchments and Coats of Arms

*Here, marzipan is rolled out and tinted with cocoa to resemble old scrolls or shields. These decorations keep well and can be prepared in advance.*

# Marzipan flowers

Marzipan is most often made into flowers, especially roses.

Marzipan flowers provide the final finishing touch to many cakes and pastries. Not only should the flowers be realistic, but they should be chosen to harmonize with the style of cake being decorated.

Often the finishing touches on the top of a pastry are what catch the eye of the consumer.

Whereas marzipan decorations do not have the finesse and detail of pulled sugar, they do have the advantage of being quick to prepare, requiring relatively little advance preparation.

If marzipan is carefully stored and protected from air (see pages 16 to 17), it can be used and shaped immediately into flowers and other decorations.

If marzipan flowers are made carefully, only a small quantity of marzipan is required, so that they are inexpensive to prepare.

**Storing Marzipan Flowers**

Marzipan flowers can be prepared ahead of time and stored in sealed tins in the same way as pulled-sugar flowers. It is imperative that they be protected from heat and humidity.

The beginning pastry chef should learn how to make roses first. Not only are roses the most frequently used in cake decorating, but once the pastry chef has mastered them, the techniques can be easily applied to other kinds of flowers.

Examples of roses and other varieties of flowers made from marzipan are shown on the following pages. A separate section is also devoted to the preparation of leaves.

# Marzipan roses

## Preparing Marzipan Roses

As mentioned on the previous pages, the rose is the most frequently prepared marzipan flower. Once the techniques of its preparation are mastered, the preparation of other flowers comes easily.

When first learning the techniques of preparing marzipan roses, it is best to start with only one method and style. Master it first before moving on to other, more complicated techniques.

**The Marzipan**

The marzipan should first be colored and then adjusted to the correct consistency (see page 16).

The marzipan should be very fine and fairly firm. Otherwise the petals of the flowers will tend to droop. (The recipe for marzipan is in volume 2, pages 96 to 99).

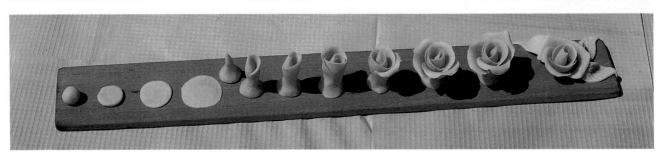

## Making the Petals

### Two Classic Methods

Rose petals are formed from half-circles of marzipan. The rounds of marzipan should be from 2 to 3 mm (about 1/8 in.) thick and have thin edges.

### a. Cutting the Half-Circles with a Knife

Use either the back of a knife or a plastic pastry scraper to cut a roll of marzipan into rounds 1.5 cm (5/8 in.) thick. These rounds should then be flattened on the pastry marble with the knife

or plastic pastry scraper, in the same way as for "fraising" pastry dough.

The rounds of marzipan are cut in half with a knife. The individual petals are then wrapped around each other or around a central base to form a rose.

### b. Thinning the Petals with a Light Bulb or Spoon

The rounds of marzipan can be worked to the proper thickness by rolling a light bulb or the back of a spoon over their surface.

They can also be covered with a sheet of plastic wrap and worked with the thumb.

### c. Other Methods

It is also possible to roll out a sheet of marzipan and cut out rounds with a cookie cutter. These rounds can then be formed to the right thickness using one of the methods suggested above.

## Constructing Marzipan Roses

Every pastry chef has his or her own special style for constructing roses and other marzipan flowers. It is difficult to give specific directions applicable to every situation. Below, however, are listed certain important rules and guidelines:

● Never let a crust form on the surface of the marzipan.

● Make sure that the pastry marble and all the tools are perfectly clean.

● Never use confectioners' sugar or starch of any kind when forming the petals or constructing the roses.

● Try to keep the petals as close to the same size as possible.

● Attach the petals so they always reach to the same height around the base.

● Make sure that each petal is securely attached to the bottom of the other

petals or to the base.

● Try to keep the flowers as even and as simple as possible. Simplicity gives the impression of greater finesse.

● Avoid forming tall flowers. Low-lying flowers give a better impression.

Practice and follow closely the procedure illustrated in the photos below.

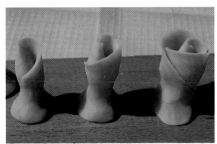

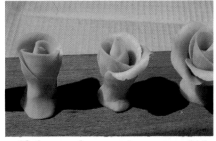

### Tips on Shaping Marzipan Roses

To construct well-shaped, realistic roses, it is necessary to form the individual flowers very carefully.

● If the petals are too thin, the rose tends to lose its shape once constructed and tends to sag.

● Do not use petals that are torn. It is better to reshape them.

● If the marzipan petals are too thick, they will be difficult to shape and will give a heavy, artificial look to the finished roses.

● It is important that the rounds of marzipan be of even thickness. The finished petals should be from 2 to 3 mm (about 1/8 in.) thick in the middle, gradually becoming extremely thin at the edges.

# Examples of marzipan roses

# Marzipan carnations

## Introduction

The techniques used for constructing marzipan carnations are considerably different than those used for making roses. Marzipan carnations are frequently used in French pastry, and their mastery is an important part of the pastry chef's craft.

Once the techniques for constructing marzipan roses have been mastered, the methods used for making carnations are easy to grasp.

The same type and consistency of marzipan is used for making carnations as for making roses. The only difference is that marzipan for roses is usually colored while that for carnations is left white. If the pastry chef wishes to color the carnations, the coloring is usually applied with a brush or sponge once the carnation is constructed. The flowers can also be sprayed with an atomizer or an airbrush (see Spraying Color, pages 70 to 71).

## Precautions

Use a very fine marzipan with no lumps. Roll it into a thin, even strip. Do not let the marzipan sit in the open air for long periods, or a crust is liable to form on its surface. Once marzipan starts to form a crust, it is very difficult to work. Never roll out the marzipan with confectioners' sugar or cornstarch.

## Procedure

Start with about 40 g (1.5 oz.) of marzipan that has been adjusted to the right consistency (see page 16).

Roll the marzipan into a rope shape 5 to 8 mm (about 1/4 in.) in diameter and 60 to 80 cm (25 to 30 in.) long. Make sure that the pastry marble is perfectly clean.

Place the rope of marzipan about 5 cm (2 in.) from the edge of the pastry marble.

Press the rope of marzipan down on the marble with a metal spatula or with the thumbs.

Continue to press down firmly on the surface of the marzipan strip with a metal

spatula or the back of a knife so that the surface is smooth and even.

Continue to work over the surface of the marzipan strip until it is about 2 mm (1/16 in.) thick. Press down firmly on the

side of the strip facing the edge of the pastry marble.

Slide the metal spatula toward the edge of the marble so that one edge of

the strip is as thin as possible.

At this point it is all right if the thinned edge is irregular and torn.

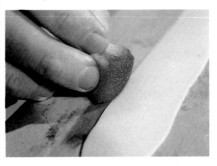

With the tip of a paring knife, cut along the beveled edge of the marzipan strip in order to give it an irregular, torn appearance (if the edge already looks this way, this step is not necessary).

Squeeze the flower about halfway up the sides to give it its final shape and hold it in place. This will divide it in two: the top side should spread out into petals and the bottom, the base, will become a solid lump.

Separate the top flower from the base.

Detach the marzipan strip from the pastry marble by quickly running a sharp paring knife beneath it.

Lift the marzipan strip, keeping the fragmented edge on the top. Fold the strip onto itself in S-shaped folds. Keep bunching up the strip in S-shaped folds until it forms a carnation of the desired size.

Make sure that the carnation is even and round before cutting off the end of the marzipan strip.

Place the marzipan carnations on parchment-paper-covered sheet pans for coloring or until needed.

Marzipan carnations should be stored under the same conditions as marzipan roses.

**Note**

It is possible to color the carnations by painting or sponging the edge of the

marzipan rope with food coloring before it is flattened with the metal spatula and folded into the final flower shape.

# Making other marzipan flowers

Once the pastry chef has mastered the construction of marzipan roses and carnations, it is easy to alter the techniques slightly to create different varieties of flowers.

Here we have demonstrated some of the more stylized varieties.

Daisies are among the simpler flowers that can be constructed with marzipan.

Usually they are cut from a sheet of marzipan with a cookie cutter. The final shaping is then completed with a small knife.

Once they are formed, the daisies are placed into round molds (egg cartons work well) and allowed to dry. Once dry, they hold their shape and are easy to assemble with sugar syrup or white chocolate.

This same technique is also used for constructing sections of more elaborate flowers such as orchids.

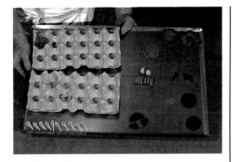

## Tulips

Tulips are made by constructing separate sections, letting them dry, and then assembling them at the end. Construct and let dry each of the following:

a. The pistil, which should be 3 to 4 cm (1 to 1.5 in.) long and 5 mm (1/4 in.) in diameter. Shape a somewhat nail-shaped tip on the top of the pistil and dip it in sugar syrup at 1260 D and then in chocolate sprinkles.

b. The base, which should be funnel shaped (see photo).

c. Oval petals, which should be worked in the same way as rose petals. The petals

should then be placed over eggs that are laid on their sides in egg cartons. The petals should be allowed to dry in this shape. The top edges of the petals should be folded back slightly.

Six petals are required to construct one tulip. Three smaller petals should be placed on the inside of the flower, with the bent upper rim facing inward. Three larger petals should be placed on the outside of the tulip, with the bent ridge facing outward.

The petals should be allowed to dry

for 48 hours before they are attached together.

First attach the pistil to the end of the funnel-shaped base with melted white chocolate. Then attach the petals to the base by first dipping them in sugar syrup at 1260 D.

Once the smaller center petals have been attached to the base, the tulip should be turned over onto a soft surface and the outer petals attached. Be sure to spread them out from the inner petals.

Allow the tulips to dry for several hours. They can then be placed on finished pastries or assembled in bouquets.

# Examples of assorted marzipan flowers

# Marzipan leaves

Marzipan leaves are relatively easy to prepare. They are used mainly to form a base around flowers and greatly improve their appearance.

Even though marzipan leaves function as a kind of backdrop for flowers placed on pastries and cakes, they are important to the final appearance of the pastry and must be prepared with great care.

Carelessly shaped, heavy-looking leaves will throw off the final appearance of finished pastries, even if the flowers and other aspects of the decoration are well executed.

On the other hand, well-formed leaves can often disguise mediocre or badly formed flowers.

Different types of leaves can be prepared, depending on the types of flowers or fruits they will accompany on the finished pastry.

**Preparation of Marzipan Leaves**

The marzipan used for the preparation of leaves should be quite stiff so that it will hold its shape. Leaves are rarely left flat when placed on a finished pastry. They are usually rounded or undulated in some way to give them a natural appearance.

Most leaves are made with pale green marzipan. They can also be given a finishing touch by brushing them with food coloring or cocoa powder.

Leaves can also be finished by brushing them with confectioners' sugar. Be sure to brush off the excess sugar at the end.

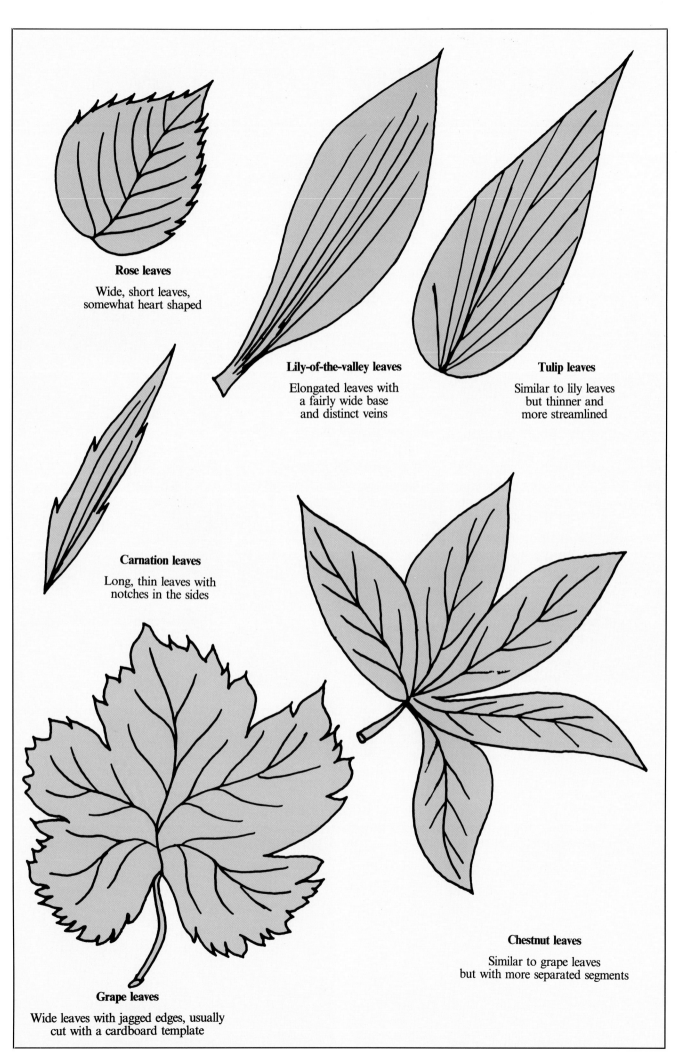

**Rose leaves**

Wide, short leaves,
somewhat heart shaped

**Lily-of-the-valley leaves**

Elongated leaves with
a fairly wide base
and distinct veins

**Tulip leaves**

Similar to lily leaves
but thinner and
more streamlined

**Carnation leaves**

Long, thin leaves with
notches in the sides

**Chestnut leaves**

Similar to grape leaves
but with more separated segments

**Grape leaves**

Wide leaves with jagged edges, usually
cut with a cardboard template

## Cutting Out the Leaves

Roll out a thin sheet of marzipan and cut out the leaves with a very sharp paring knife.

Thin the edges of each leaf by pressing them with a finger, light bulb, metal spatula, or plastic pastry scraper. This gives a delicate look to the leaves without making them too thin, which would cause them to sag after being mounted on the finished pastries.

Once the edges have been thinned and smoothed, the leaves can be brushed with cocoa powder or food coloring.

## Forming the Veins

Indent veins on the surface of the leaves by gently pressing them with the back of a knife or the edge of a plastic pastry scraper.

The veins covering the surface of marzipan leaves can be more or less elabo-

rate, depending on the type of leaf and style of presentation.

Once the veins have been applied to the leaves, the leaves should be rounded into their final shapes.

They should then be placed on sheet pans and allowed to harden so they maintain their shape once placed on the finished cake or pastry.

Marzipan leaves can be prepared in advance and sealed in containers with tight-fitting lids. They can then be used as needed.

# Inscriptions on marzipan parchment

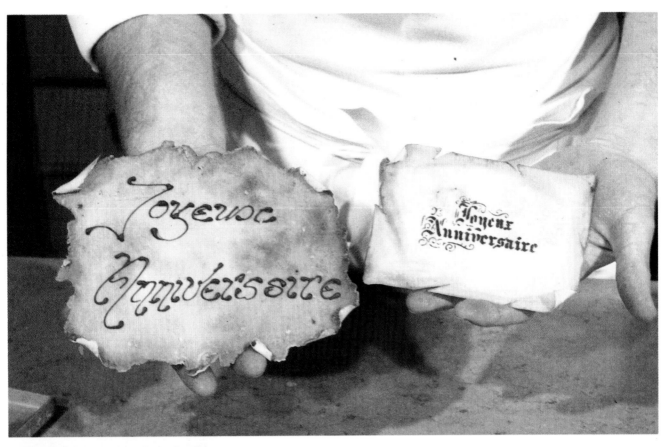

## Adding a Personal Touch to Finished Cakes

Marzipan can be rolled out and decorated to resemble old parchment. These "parchment" sheets can be made in advance and decorated with inscriptions as they are needed.

Marzipan parchments can be made in a variety of shapes and sizes. They are convenient for the pastry chef, who can write inscriptions on the surface of the parchment and apply them to finished cakes as needed.

# Preparing Marzipan Parchments

Roll plain, uncolored marzipan into a 2-mm-thick (1/16–in.) sheet on the pastry marble. The marzipan should be quite firm. Cut the sheet of marzipan into the desired shape.

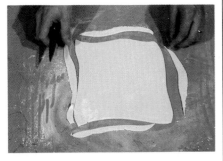

Cut the edges of the marzipan in an irregular way with the paring knife.

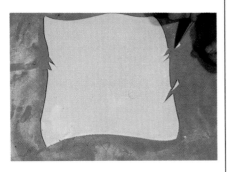

Thin the edges of the marzipan by pressing several times with the palm or heel of the hand. This gives a fine, irregular look to the edges without thinning the center, which would make the marzipan sheets too fragile and difficult to work with.

The edges of the marzipan are given an antiqued effect by rubbing them with cocoa powder. The cocoa powder should be dark at the edges and gradually fade toward the center.

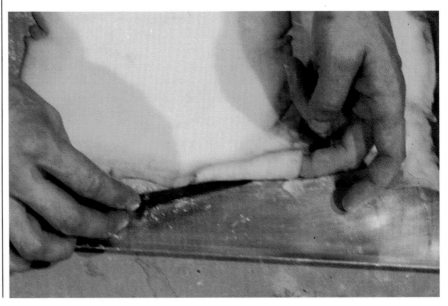

To apply the cocoa powder, keep a small container on the marble near the sheet of marzipan being prepared. Coat the edges of the marzipan with the cocoa, using a fingertip or pastry brush. Coat the thinned edges of the marzipan first and then work gradually toward the center.

Smooth off the cocoa powder so the surface is perfectly even.

*Note:* Once the excess cocoa powder has been brushed off the surface of the marzipan, the color can be darkened by simply rubbing over the cocoa powder with the tip of a wet finger. The corners of the marzipan parchment can be curled up over themselves with a paring knife to give an antique look.

Once completed, the marzipan parchments should be placed on sheet pans that have been sprinkled with confectioners' sugar.

Leave the parchments in the open air for several hours so they dry and become firm.

Once the marzipan parchments have dried, they can be saved and written on as needed.

Marzipan parchments can be saved for several weeks, but it is important that they be protected from humidity, heat, and dust.

It is also possible to give an antique look to the marzipan parchments by lightly burning them with a propane torch. Gently wave the tip of the flame over the part of the parchment to be antiqued while working inward from the outer edges.

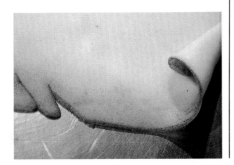

# Marzipan sculpture

## Introduction

This section discusses methods for working marzipan into decorative shapes. The techniques range from simple to quite complex.

Shaping marzipan is not as difficult as it sometimes looks. It is important, however, to pay careful attention to the texture of the marzipan and to use food coloring for marzipan fruit judiciously.

Although marzipan fruit and animals are frequently used to decorate finished cakes and pastries, they can also be sold by themselves. In France, they provide considerable supplemental income for pastry shops. They keep for several weeks so they can be prepared during periods when business is slow.

Because marzipan sculptures are usually sold individually, it is important that they be of even weight—a bunch of five cherries should weigh the same as a banana, a mouse the same as an elephant.

Marzipan sculpture is almost always executed with plain uncolored marzipan. The coloring is usually applied after the marzipan is shaped, with a sponge, pastry brush, or fingertip.

Food coloring can also be applied to marzipan sculptures with an atomizer. This method makes it easier to apply delicate shading to give a natural look to the sculptures.

The airbrush is now being used more frequently by pastry chefs. Even though it is somewhat more expensive to apply colors in this way, the technique offers several advantages. The technique is fast and can be used to coat finished marzipan sculptures with cocoa butter, which helps them stay fresher longer.

The following pages contain photographs of marzipan fruit and vegetables and animals.

The fruit and vegetables are shown with coloring, while the animals are shown plain so it is easier to see the methods used for shaping.

When coloring marzipan fruit and vegetables, it is best to try to duplicate their natural colors, but when coloring animals, a bit of cartoonish fantasy is of course permitted.

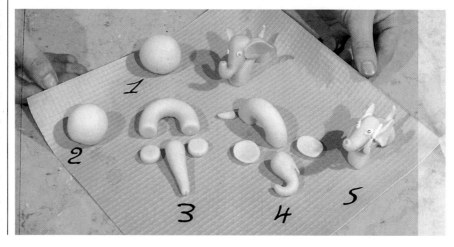

### Note

Marzipan can be sculpted and shaped without the use of special equipment; a paring knife and scissors are frequently the only tools required. Nevertheless, many pastry chefs like to have on hand a series of little plastic or wooden tools (see photo) which can be used to make lines, indentations, and other forms.

### Preparing the Marzipan

Make sure that the marzipan is firm but not crusty or granular. If necessary, work it on the marble to smooth it and make it more malleable.

Weigh the marzipan into sections large enough for a batch of miniature sculptures. About 400 g (14 oz.) is a good size to use.

Form the marzipan into an even roll, which can then be divided into 50-g (1.5-oz.) sections for shaping.

It is always a good idea to roll each of the sections into balls before beginning the shaping.

Depending on the type of sculpture being executed, the small sections of marzipan can be broken into smaller sections to form the various parts of the final shape.

### Example: Elephant

(See photo, page 130)

Divide the ball of marzipan into two equal balls of 25 g (1 oz.) each.

1. One ball forms the body.

2. The second ball should be divided a second time to provide the head, the trunk, two ears, and the tail.

3. Each of these sections should be shaped separately.

4. When each of the sections has the correct shape, the elephant should be put together with sugar syrup containing glucose at 1260 D (see box at right).

Always use a clean work surface when working with marzipan. Also be sure that hands and all tools are perfectly clean. Never use confectioners' sugar or starch of any kind on the work surface.

### Shaping Marzipan Balls

Marzipan balls are best formed between the palms of the hands. Hold one hand still while rotating the marzipan with the other.

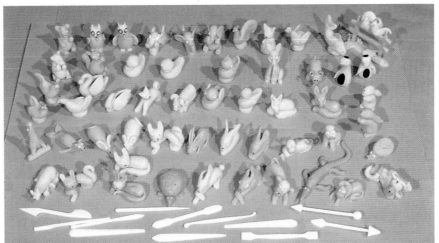

When forming oval shapes, move one of the hands to-and-fro rather than with a circular motion.

When shaping marzipan into cones, use a back-and-forth movement with the top hand held at an angle over the bottom one.

When rolling marzipan into logs, work directly on the pastry marble.

Once the marzipan has been formed into these basic shapes, it is given its final form with the pastry chef's miniature tools. The individual parts to the sculptures are then pieced together with the glucose sugar syrup.

### Sugar Syrup

1 L water (34 fl. oz.)
1 kg sugar (35 oz.)
500 g glucose (17.5 oz.)

Boil the ingredients together for 1 minute. Use the syrup only when it is cool.

Lightly moisten the sections of the sculpture with the syrup. Do not use too much.

Let the syrup dry in the open air for 12 to 24 hours before applying the coloring.

121

# Examples of marzipan fruits

# Examples of marzipan fruits

# Examples of marzipan vegetables

### Vegetables

*It is often helpful for the beginning pastry chef to have an actual model of the vegetable being shaped.*

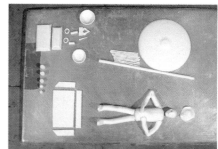

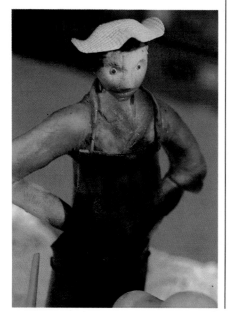

# Examples of marzipan vegetables

# Examples of marzipan animals

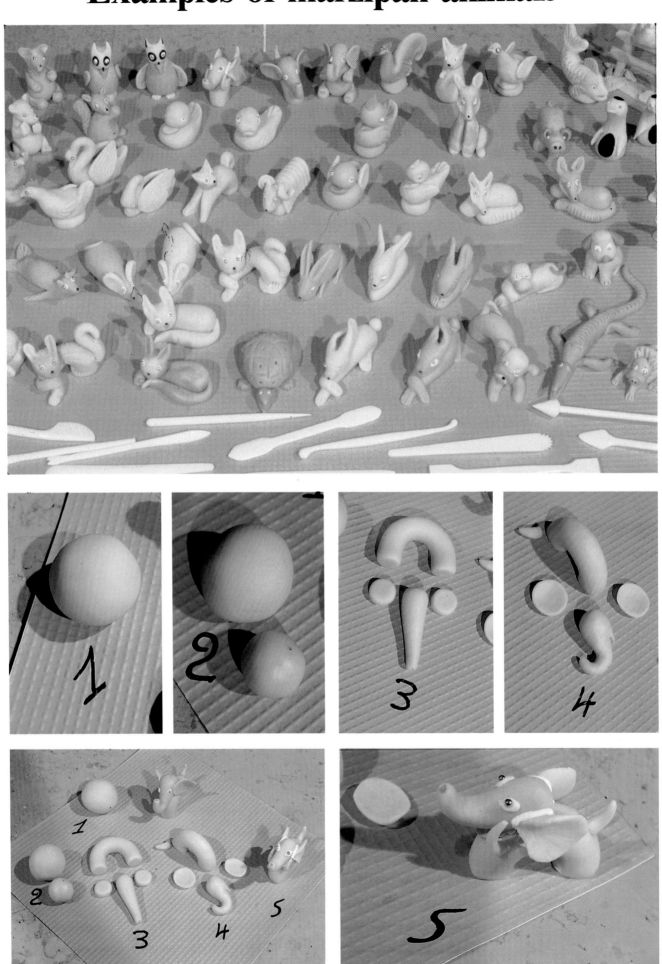

131

# Examples of marzipan animals

133

# Examples of marzipan animals

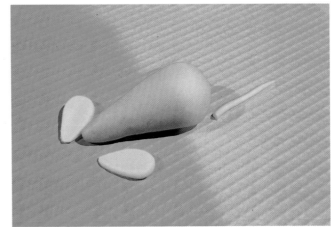

# Examples of marzipan animals

# Examples of marzipan animals

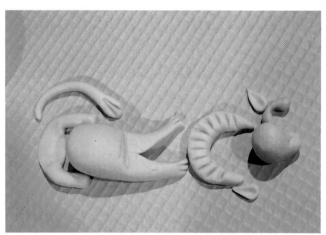

# Chapter 4
# Examples of professional decoration

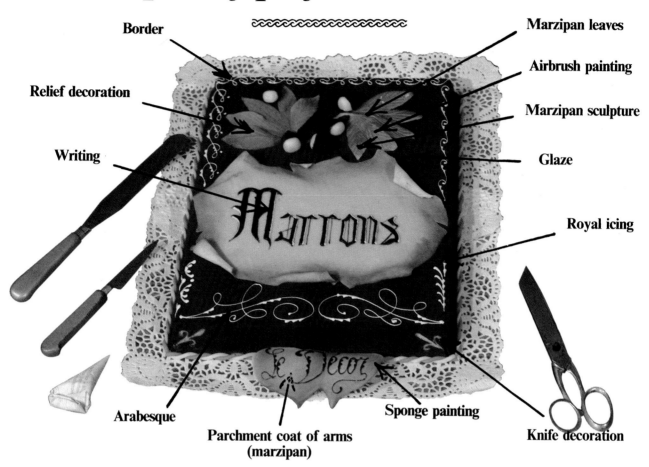

Border

Marzipan leaves

Relief decoration

Airbrush painting

Marzipan sculpture

Writing

Glaze

Royal icing

Arabesque

Sponge painting

Parchment coat of arms
(marzipan)

Knife decoration

*Basic cake decorating requires the use of certain standard techniques. Once these techniques have been mastered, cakes and other pastries can be decorated according to the whim of the pastry chef.*

*In a sophisticated pastry shop, the pastry chef is frequently called upon to design specially decorated cakes and pastries. Remember that a well-designed cake is often the crowning glory of even the most elaborate meal. It is often with the dessert that a meal is given its distinction, especially when celebrating special events.*

*The repertoire of cakes is divided into three categories. Each represents a different level of difficulty and places different demands on the creativity and talents of the pastry chef.*

## Cakes and Pastries for Special Occasions

*1. Standard holidays and feast days*

*2. Special-order cakes for standard special occasions*

*3. Special-order cakes for specific special events*

# Decorating styles for special occasions

## 1. Standard Holidays and Feast Days

These are standard occasions for which specially decorated cakes are required. Valentine's Day, New Year's Day, Christmas, and Easter are examples.

Even though the decorations for these cakes are fairly standardized, the pastry chef should always keep in mind that cakes should change according to the season. This is also an important sales tactic for pastry shops that display their cakes and pastries in the front window.

Because demand for cakes increases around holidays, it is possible for the pastry chef to foresee demand to some degree and prepare some of the special decorations in advance. For this reason, simple decorations that can be made ahead of time and stored should be used.

It is often during periods when the demand for cakes and pastries is the greatest that the customer looking for a special cake or pastry is liable to compare the merits of each pastry shop's cakes.

It is especially important during these periods that the pastry chef do his or her best to excel.

The pastry chef should devise a variety of styles and decorations for each occasion so the customer has a wide enough array to choose from. Since annual occasions are anticipated in advance, the pastry chef is rarely called upon to prepare custom-prepared and decorated cakes during these periods.

## 2. Special-order Cakes for Standard Special Occasions

These cakes are custom-ordered by customers who want to celebrate a special, yet personal occasion, such as a birthday, baptism, wedding, or engagement.

They place greater demand on the pastry chef because it is necessary to prepare the cakes specially, following the wishes of the customer.

Usually, however, the pastry chef is already familiar with certain standard types of decoration that are appropriate to the specific occasion.

Some of these special cakes are easily customized by the pastry chef.

For example, a cake prepared to celebrate an engagement can be simply decorated by writing "Congratulations" in the center with hearts or birds drawn on the surface with a paper cone. The names of the engaged couple can then be written in each corner.

A cake such as this presents little trouble for the experienced pastry chef and can be produced with little additional expense.

It is, of course, possible to prepare more elaborate cakes for the same types of occasions. An example for an engagement would be to decorate the surface of the cake with an elaborate sugar butterfly resting on pulled-sugar flowers, with the couple's names written on marzipan parchment.

Elaborate cakes such as this represent considerable time and expense. Their price should be carefully discussed with the customer beforehand to avoid any confusion. The pastry chef should also remember not to promise cakes that are beyond the abilities of his or her staff.

## 3. Special-order Cakes for Specific Special Events

These cakes must be prepared for special occasions for which there are no standardized rules of style. For this reason, the customer must depend entirely on the creativity, imagination, and good taste of the pastry chef. The finished cake must be entirely original and unique. Such cakes are usually quite elaborate and make use of a wide variety of special decorating techniques, such as use of a paper cone, marzipan decorations, use of the pastry bag and airbrush, pastillage, and possibly pulled-sugar decorations and painting with food coloring.

These special cakes are often prepared over a period of several days so that the various elements can be prepared and set aside until the final construction of the cake. The pastry chef should carefully consider the use of each element as well as the final appearance of the cake before embarking on these time-consuming projects.

First of all, the pastry chef should consult carefully with the customer to

discuss his or her requirements and budget. Once the wishes of the customer have been established, the pastry chef needs to consider carefully a wide range of factors, such as the time required, the complexity of the decoration, the profit margin, the presentation, the stability of the cake if it is to be served outside or in a hot place, and finally the delivery.

When consulting with the customer, it is important that he or she be given a range of choices, which will dictate the final complexity and expense of the cake.

Three levels can be proposed:

- simple decoration with a paper cone or pastry bag
- more elaborate decoration with marzipan parchment and marzipan or pulled-sugar flowers
- elaborate decoration using pastillage, cocoa painting, and marzipan or pulled-sugar flowers.

Once these parameters are clear, the pastry chef can go about making a mental design of the cake and establishing a final price. It is then recommended to have a second meeting with the customer, during which the plan and final price can be discussed. If necessary, the proposed cake can then be modified.

Once the plan for the special cake has been established, the pastry chef can then go about organizing the work. Some of the decorations, such as pastillage, need to be prepared as far in advance as possible so they have time to set and dry. Other decorations that do not spoil, such as sugar flowers and marzipan leaves, should also be prepared well in advance. Since these special decorations do not spoil, plenty of time can be allotted to their preparation. This makes the pastry chef's schedule more flexible in case there are any problems.

These special-ordered cakes provide helpful challenges to pastry chefs and allow them to develop and perfect their imagination and skills.

## Examples

### *Photos on next page*

| | |
|---|---|
| **Marzipan decorations** | **Cocoa powder coating** |
| **Marzipan leaves** | **Marzipan parchment** |
| **Border with paper cone** | **Arabesque with paper cone** |
| **Knife scratching** | **Braided marzipan** |
| **Writing** | **Capital letters** |

# "Bonne fête" (holidays and birthdays)

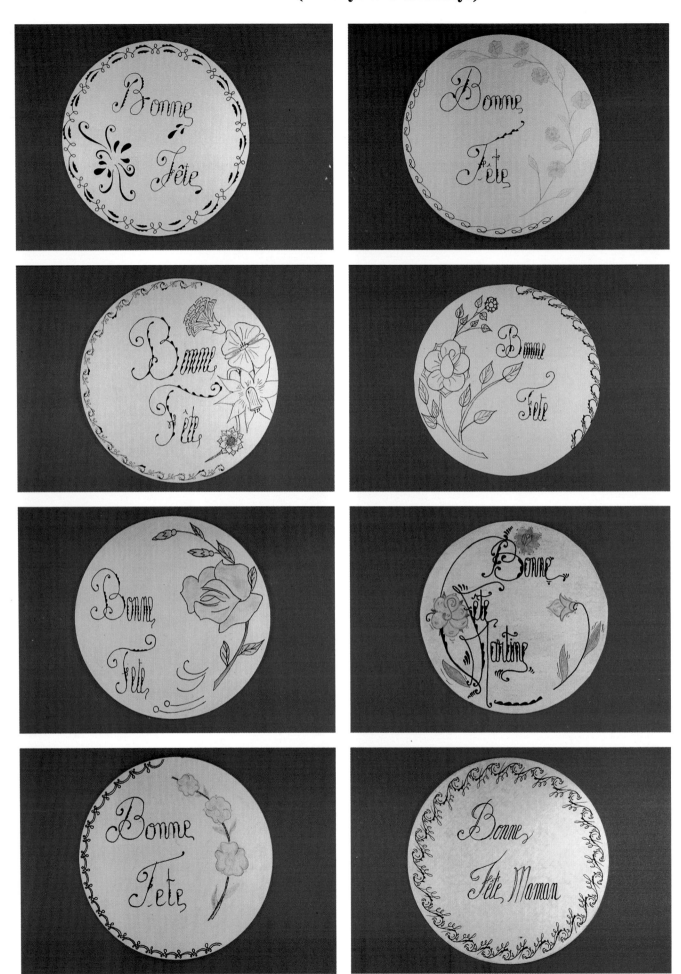

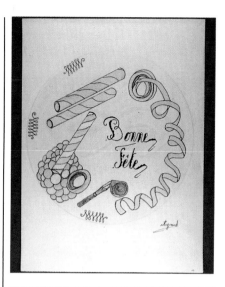

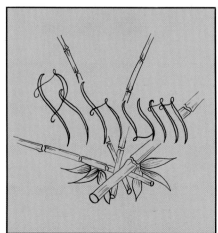

# Baptême et fiançailles (Baptisms and engagements)

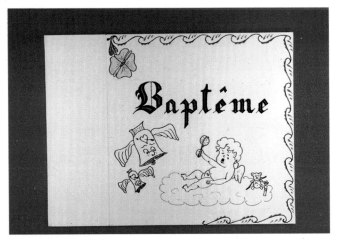

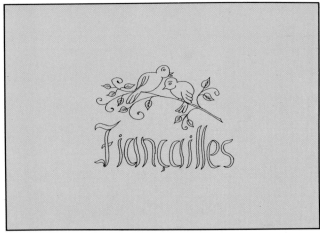

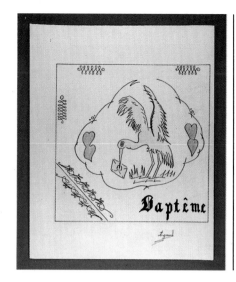

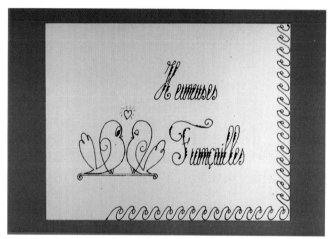

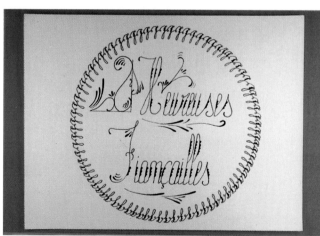
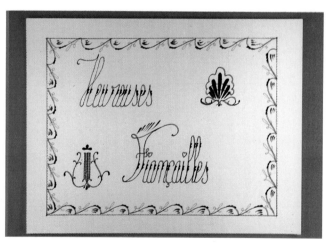

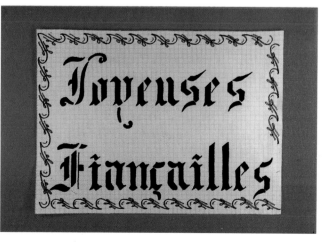

# Mariage et noces d'or (Weddings and golden anniversaries)

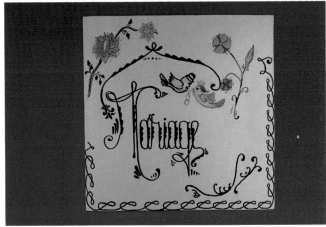

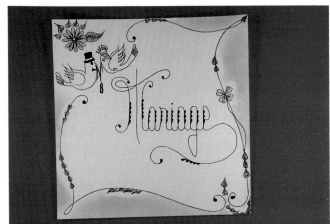

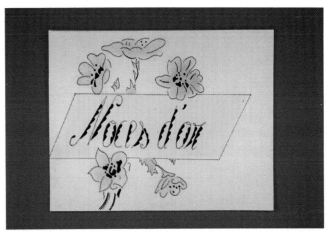
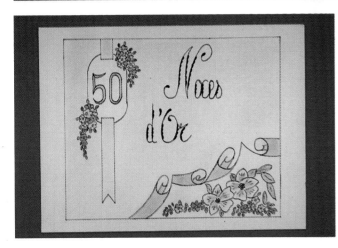

# Carnaval (Mardi Gras)

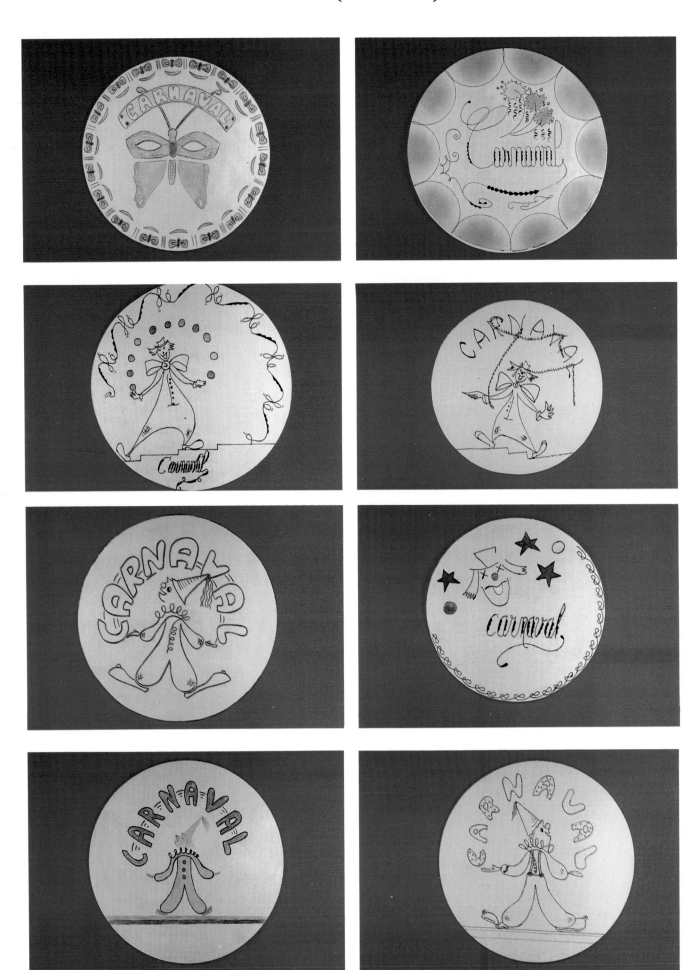

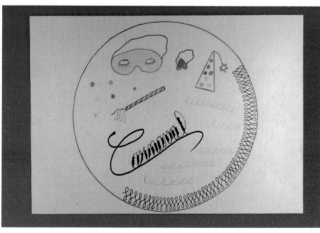

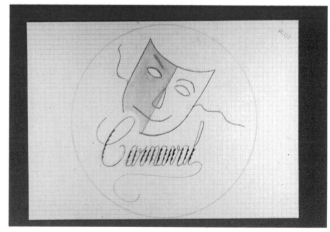

149

# Noël, nouvel an, anniversaires, Sainte-Catherine

# (Christmas, New Year's, anniversaries, and Saint Catherine's Day)

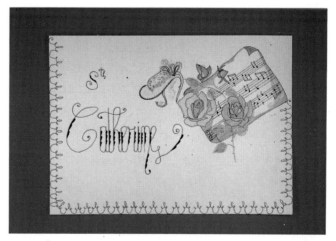

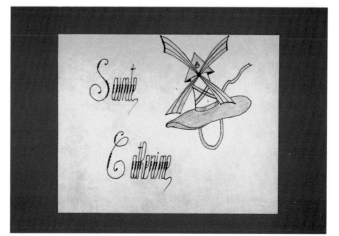

# Chapter 5

# *Modern Desserts*

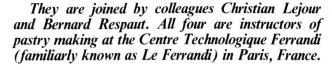

This chapter is dedicated to modern desserts and the various techniques and presentations that go into making them.

Many of the cakes presented in this chapter are constructed from different elements and are assembled in a metal cake ring. Most of the desserts can be stored in the freezer until needed. It is best to finish decorating the cakes as they are used, especially when they decorated with chocolate or fresh fruit.

Eight eminent pastry chefs were chosen to provide a collection of desserts to demonstrate a diversity of styles and techniques.

The first four pastry chefs include the two authors of this series, Roland Bilheux and Alain Escoffier.

They are joined by colleagues Christian Lejour and Bernard Respaut. All four are instructors of pastry making at the Centre Technologique Ferrandi (familiarly known as Le Ferrandi) in Paris, France.

The other four equally accomplished pastry chefs, known throughout France as well as internationally, are: François Bastien, Denis Ruffel, Henri Raimbault, and Jean Creveux.

The desserts in this chapter are representative of the variety and creativity possible in the field of pastry making once basic techniques, as shown in this series, are mastered and combined with professional experience.

**Roland Bilheux**

Pomme Normande
Marrons Whisky
Tulipes Passion
Orange Kiwi
Mousse Mandarine/Poire/
 Caramel
4/21 Chocolat/Pistache
Ombre et Lumière
Le Mogador

**Alain Escoffier**

Désir Rose
Le Crèspuscule
Le Stanislas
Caprice aux Poires
Le Petit Bonheur
Miroir Citron/Chocolat
Charlotte Alliance

**Christian Lejour**

Longchamp
Rafraîchissant
Chantilly
L'Antillais
Prestige Passion Framboises
Perlia
Délice Poire Caramel
Cardinal Cassis

**Bernard Respaut**

Rêve des Iles
Irish Coffee
Le Rucher
Le Sicilien
Sao Paulo
Black is Weett
Coeur Fidèle
Spanish Orange
Le Rêve de Montmorency

**François Bastien**

Le Nougat de Tours
Le Trocadéro
Le Montmartre
Le Brésilien

**Denis Ruffel**

Vallée d'Auge
Méli-Mélo
Mille-feuilles de Fruits Rouges
Charlotte au Chocolat

**Henri Raimbault**

La Chocolette
Le Saint-Galhais

**Jean Creveux**

Miroir de Printemps
Miroir d'Eté
Miroir d'Automne
Miroir d'Hiver

# A guide to

The following eight pages make up a sort of catalog of the desserts presented in this chapter, including a photograph of the finished product, a sketch of the construction of each dessert, and the page where it can be found in the book.

The text following this catalog has a more detailed photograph of the finished product, a side view of a cut portion, and often a close-up of detail work. A recipe and procedure is given for each dessert. The photograph may vary slightly from the procedure given for assembling the desserts; this is to encourage the reader to alter or enhance the decoration and assembly of the cakes so as to personalize them.

(Pomme Normande)

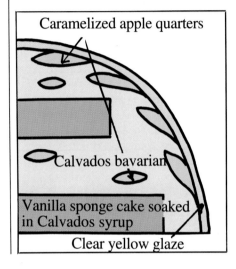

Caramelized apple quarters

Calvados bavarian

Vanilla sponge cake soaked in Calvados syrup

Clear yellow glaze

(Marrons Whisky)

(Tulipes Passion)

(Orange Kiwi)

Light ganache glaze

| Chestnut/whiskey bavarian plus chestnut pieces |
| Coconut-hazelnut sponge cake |
| Chestnut/whiskey bavarian plus chestnut pieces |
| Coconut-hazelnut sponge cake |

Almond craquelées (optional)

Assorted-fruit garnish

Passion-fruit mousse

Tulip-base

Kiwi slices

| Almond sponge cake soaked in Cointreau syrup |
| Orange mousse |
| Almond sponge cake soaked in Cointreau syrup |
| Orange mousse |

Candied orange slices

# assembling the desserts

(Mousse Mandarine/Poire/Caramel)

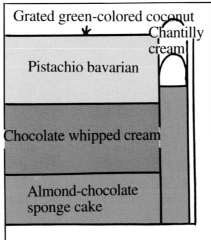

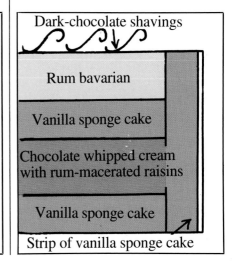

(4/21 Chocolat/Pistache)

(Ombre et Lumière)

Small white-chocolate shavings

| Mandarin mousse |
| Chocolate génoise |
| Mandarin mousse | Vanilla/choc. sponge cake |
| Chocolate génoise | |

Caramelized pear quarters

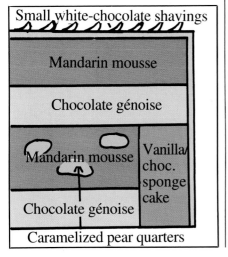

Grated green-colored coconut

Chantilly cream

| Pistachio bavarian |
| Chocolate whipped cream |
| Almond-chocolate sponge cake |

Dark-chocolate shavings

| Rum bavarian |
| Vanilla sponge cake |
| Chocolate whipped cream with rum-macerated raisins |
| Vanilla sponge cake |

Strip of vanilla sponge cake

(Le Mogador)

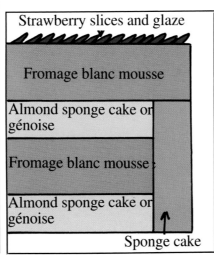

(Désir Rose)

(Le Crépuscule)

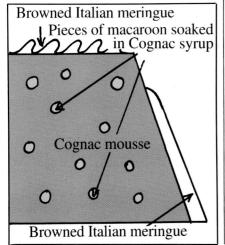

Browned Italian meringue
Pieces of macaroon soaked in Cognac syrup

Cognac mousse

Browned Italian meringue

Strawberry slices and glaze

| Fromage blanc mousse |
| Almond sponge cake or génoise |
| Fromage blanc mousse |
| Almond sponge cake or génoise |

Sponge cake

Chocolate shavings

| Chocolate mousse |
| Vanilla bavarian |
| Génoise |

Ladyfingers

# A guide to

(Le Stanislas)

(Caprice aux Poires)

(Le Petit Bonheur)

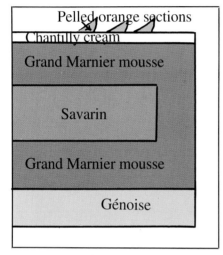

Pelled orange sections
Chantilly cream
Grand Marnier mousse
Savarin
Grand Marnier mousse
Génoise

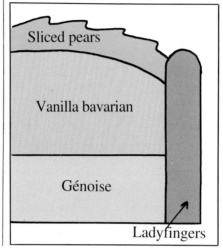

Sliced pears
Vanilla bavarian
Génoise
Ladyfingers

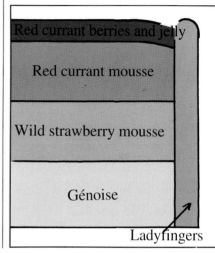

Red currant berries and jelly
Red currant mousse
Wild strawberry mousse
Génoise
Ladyfingers

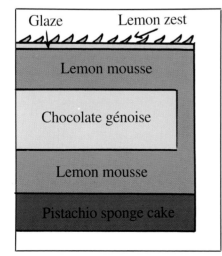

(Miroir Citron/chocolat)

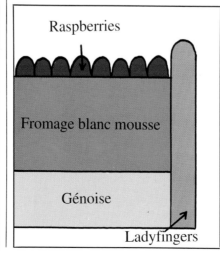

(Charlotte Alliance)

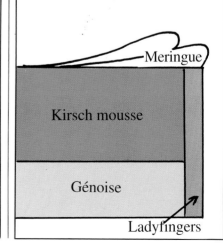

(Longchamp)

Glaze          Lemon zest
Lemon mousse
Chocolate génoise
Lemon mousse
Pistachio sponge cake

Raspberries
Fromage blanc mousse
Génoise
Ladyfingers

Meringue
Kirsch mousse
Génoise
Ladyfingers

# assembling the desserts

(Rafraîchissant)

(Chantilly)

(L'Antillais)

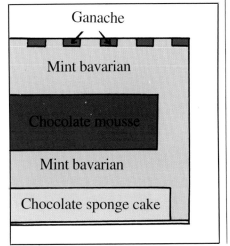

Ganache

Mint bavarian

Chocolate mousse

Mint bavarian

Chocolate sponge cake

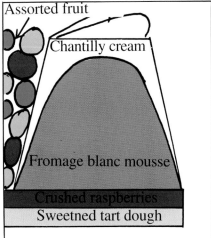

Assorted fruit

Chantilly cream

Fromage blanc mousse

Crushed raspberries

Sweetned tart dough

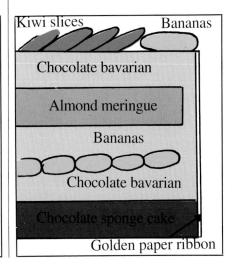

Kiwi slices     Bananas

Chocolate bavarian

Almond meringue

Bananas

Chocolate bavarian

Chocolate sponge cake

Golden paper ribbon

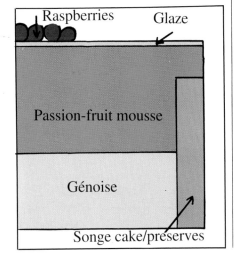

(Prestige Passion Framboise)

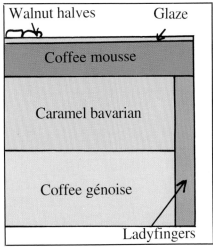

(Perlia)

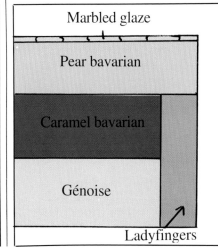

(Délice Poire Caramel)

Raspberries     Glaze

Passion-fruit mousse

Génoise

Songe cake/préserves

Walnut halves     Glaze

Coffee mousse

Caramel bavarian

Coffee génoise

Ladyfingers

Marbled glaze

Pear bavarian

Caramel bavarian

Génoise

Ladyfingers

# A guide to

(Cardinal Cassis)

Black currant glaze

Black currant mousse

Génoise

Black currant mousse

Meringue

Chocolate shavings

(Rêve des Iles)

Sprayed chocolate covering

Chocolatine cream

Rum bavarian

Chocolate sponge-cake

Raisins macerated in rum

(Irish Coffee)

Coffee fondant

Coffee bavrian

Coffee génoise

Light coffee cream

Coffee génoise

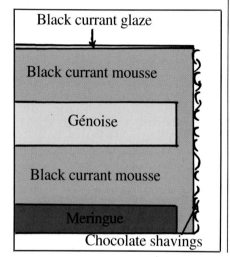

(Le Rucher)

Raspberry mousse

Honey bavarian

Raspberry mousse

Honey sponge cake

Honey bavarian

Honey sponge cake

Raspberry mousse

Honey sponge cake

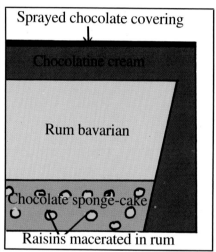

(Le Sicilien)

Nut brittle

Pistachio mousse

Pistachio macaroon

Pear bavarian

Pistachio macaroon

Pistachio mousse

Pistachio macaroon

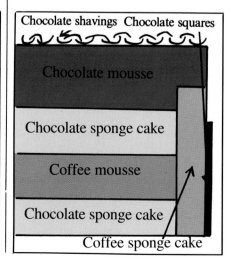

(Sao Paulo)

Chocolate shavings   Chocolate squares

Chocolate mousse

Chocolate sponge cake

Coffee mousse

Chocolate sponge cake

Coffee sponge cake

# assembling the desserts

(Black is Weett)

(Coeur fidèle)

(Spanish Orange)

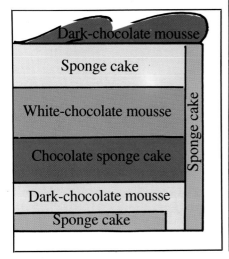

Dark-chocolate mousse
Sponge cake
White-chocolate mousse
Chocolate sponge cake
Dark-chocolate mousse
Sponge cake
Sponge cake

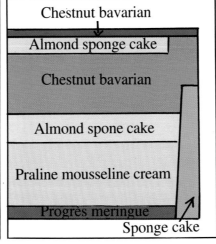

Chestnut bavarian
Almond sponge cake
Chestnut bavarian
Almond spone cake
Praline mousseline cream
Progrès meringue
Sponge cake

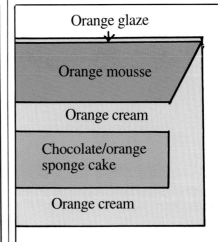

Orange glaze
Orange mousse
Orange cream
Chocolate/orange sponge cake
Orange cream

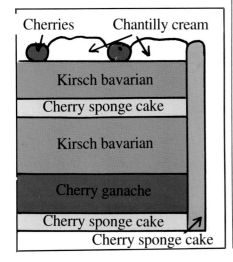

(Le Rêve de Montmorency)

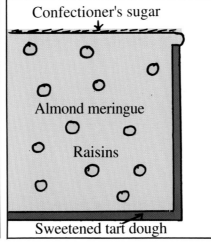

(Le Nougat de Tours)

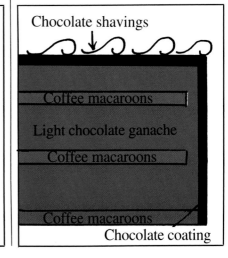

(Le Trocadéro)

Cherries   Chantilly cream
Kirsch bavarian
Cherry sponge cake
Kirsch bavarian
Cherry ganache
Cherry sponge cake
Cherry sponge cake

Confectioner's sugar
Almond meringue
Raisins
Sweetened tart dough

Chocolate shavings
Coffee macaroons
Light chocolate ganache
Coffee macaroons
Coffee macaroons
Chocolate coating

# A guide to

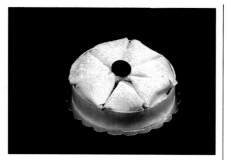

(Le Montmartre)

(Le Brésilien)

(Vallée d'Auge)

White-chocolate shavings

Chocolate mousse

Chocolate meringue

Chocolate mousse

Chocolate meringue

White-chocolate coating

Coffee macaroons

Coffee mousse

Coffee meringues

Coffee mousse

Chocolate meringue

Coffee macaroons

Glaze  Apple slices

Apple mousse

Apple mousse

Almond sponge cake

Prune-coated sponge cake

(Méli-Mélo)

(Mille-feuilles de Fruits Rouges)

(Charlotte au Chocolat)

Tropical fruit

Almond spone cake

Tropical bavarian

Fruit

Tropical bavarian

Chocolate-covered almond succès

Red fruit and puff pastry

Puff pastry

Honey mousseline

Raspberries and strawberries

Honey mousseline

Puff pastry

Strawberry halves

White chocolate

Chocolate shavings

Chocolate bavarian

Sponge cake

Vanilla + chocolate sponge cake

# assembling the desserts

(La Chocolette)

(Miroir de Printemps)

(Miroir d'été)

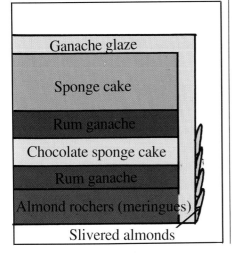

| Ganache glaze |
| Sponge cake |
| Rum ganache |
| Chocolate sponge cake |
| Rum ganache |
| Almond rochers (meringues) |

Slivered almonds

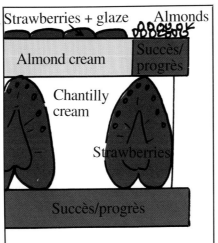

Strawberries + glaze — Almonds

Almond cream — Succès/progrès

Chantilly cream

Strawberries

Succès/progrès

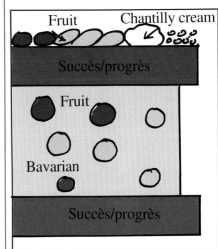

Fruit — Chantilly cream

Succès/progrès

Fruit

Bavarian

Succès/progrès

(Le Saint-Galhais)

(Miroir d'Automne)

(Miroir d'Hiver)

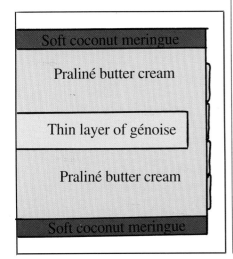

| Soft coconut meringue |
| Praliné butter cream |
| Thin layer of génoise |
| Praliné butter cream |
| Soft coconut meringue |

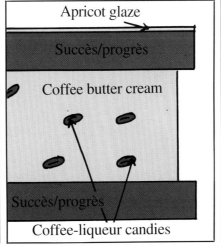

Apricot glaze

Succès/progrès

Coffee butter cream

Succès/progrès

Coffee-liqueur candies

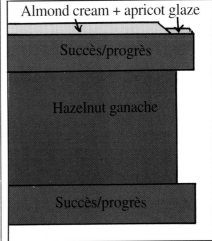

Almond cream + apricot glaze

Succès/progrès

Hazelnut ganache

Succès/progrès

# Modern desserts by Roland Bilheux

## Roland Bilheux

*Roland Bilheux, as co-author of the* Professional French Pastry Series, *has already displayed his knowledge of pastry.*

*His creative talents are shown in the desserts on the following pages.*

*Originally from Mayenne, the midwestern region of France, Bilheux has combined classical pastry making with a somewhat modern approach.*

*This combination makes for attractive and appetizing desserts.*

# Pomme Normande

## Presentation

The pomme Normande is given a dome shape, an unusual and attractive way of presenting this dessert, requiring a bombe mold or other round, semispherical mold.

The pomme Normande can be made with local and seasonal fruit, such as pears, plums, and mandarins.

## Composition

Vanilla sponge cake
Calvados bavarian
Caramelized apples
Calvados-flavored sugar syrup
Light glaze (such as apricot)

## Recipe

For 35 to 40 servings. 3 half-sphere bombe molds, 20 cm (8 in.) in diameter

## Vanilla Sponge Cake

From a sheet of vanilla sponge cake, cut three circles, each 18 cm (7 in.) in diameter, and three circles 10 cm (4 in.) in diameter.

## Caramelized Apples

Cut 9 apples into quarters. Caramelize by sautéing with 50 g (1.5 oz.) of sugar and 25 g (1 oz.) of butter; flambé with 25 ml (1 fl. oz.) of Calvados.

## Calvados Bavarian

750 ml milk (25 fl. oz.)
300 g sugar (10.5 oz.)
10 egg yolks
12 sheets (24 g) gelatin (3/4 oz.)
750 ml cream (25 fl. oz.), whipped
100 ml aged Calvados (3.5 fl. oz.)

## Glaze

Apricot jelly heated and thinned with a little Calvados and several drops of vanilla extract.

## Assembling the Cake

Butter the mold with clarified butter.
Line the mold with the caramelized apple quarters.
Fill the mold halfway with the Calvados bavarian. Add a layer of sponge cake soaked in Calvados-flavored sugar syrup at 1260 D. Repeat to fill the mold.
Apples may be placed in the bavarian if desired.
Place the cake in the freezer to set.

## Decoration

Brush the cake with the glaze. Highlight the cake by spraying it with red and green food coloring, using an atomizer. Place one or two leaves made of pulled sugar or marzipan on the top of the cake.

# Marrons whisky

## Presentation

The marrons whisky cake is usually made during winter months, when fresh chestnuts are available. Commercially, the food cost of this cake is quite reasonable. The marrons whisky cake is strongly flavored with liquor and would be appropriate at the end of a special meal.

## Composition

Coconut/hazelnut sponge cake
Whiskey/chestnut bavarian
Pieces of glazed chestnuts macerated in whiskey
Whiskey-flavored sugar syrup
Light ganache
Threads of white chocolate plus chestnuts and leaves made from marzipan (decoration)

## Recipe

For 35 to 40 servings

### Coconut/Hazelnut Sponge Cake

For 10 round bases, 22 cm (8.5 in.) in diameter

250 ml milk (8.5 fl. oz.), brought to a boil and poured over 250 g grated coconut (9 oz.)
500 g praline paste (17.5 oz.)
6 eggs - 50 g cake flour (1.5 oz.)
8 egg whites, beaten to firm peaks, plus 100 g sugar (3.5 oz.) to firm the whites

Mix all the ingredients together, except for the egg whites, which have been beaten with the sugar. Then carefully fold the whites into the mixture.

Place the mixture in a tart ring set on a sheet pan covered with buttered parchment paper. Fill the rings with a layer 5 to 8 mm (about 1/4 in.) high. Bake in a moderate oven at 200°C (375°F).

### Chestnut/Whisky Bavarian

500 ml milk (17 fl. oz.)
200 g sugar (7 oz.)
8 egg yolks
700 g chestnut puree (24.5 oz.)
12 sheets (24 g) gelatin (3/4 oz.)
750 ml cream (25 fl. oz.), whipped
100 ml whiskey (3.5 fl. oz.)

### Macerated Chestnut Pieces

500 g glazed chestnut pieces (17.5 oz.), macerated in 100 ml whiskey (3.5 fl. oz.) in an airtight container for a minimum of 3 days, and up to 10 days if possible.

### Whiskey-flavored Sugar Syrup

250 ml sugar syrup (8.5 fl. oz.), at 1260 D
100 ml whiskey (3.5 fl. oz.)

### Light Ganache Glaze

250 ml milk (8.5 fl. oz.)
350 g milk-chocolate couverture (12.5 oz.)
150 g dark-chocolate couverture (5 oz.)

### White-Chocolate Decorations

Shape the chestnuts out of marzipan and dip them in tempered white-chocolate couverture or white-chocolate coating (pâte à glacer), a type of chocolate that does not need to be tempered to become firm after melting. Cut and shape the leaves out of marzipan. With a knife, cut grooves in the leaves to create veins, then cover the leaves with cocoa powder and brush off the excess to highlight the veins.

### Assembling the Cake

Place a cake ring that is 4 to 5 cm (1.5 to 2 in.) high over a cardboard circle. Inside the ring, place a layer of coconut/hazelnut sponge cake that is slightly smaller in diameter than the cake ring, and brush with whiskey-flavored sugar syrup.

Fill the ring halfway with a layer of chestnut/whiskey bavarian.

Sprinkle the bavarian with pieces of macerated glazed chestnut.

Place a layer of coconut/hazelnut sponge cake atop the bavarian and brush it with whiskey-flavored sugar syrup. Place a second layer of bavarian, thinner than the first, on top of the sponge cake and sprinkle it with the macerated chestnut pieces.

Fill the cake to the rim with the bavarian.

Allow the cake to set in the freezer.

After the cake is set, glaze it with light ganache, using a metal spatula. Decorate the ganache quickly, before it sets, by piping on thin lines of white chocolate with a paper cone.

Remove the metal cake ring by warming it, wrapping a hot towel around the outside for several seconds.

### Decoration

Place the marzipan leaves and chestnuts on top of the cake.

# Tulipes passion

## Presentation

The tulipes passion is an original and attractive dessert, especially light, refreshing, and appealing to those who enjoy tart fruits such as kiwi and passion fruit.

The tulipes passion cannot be held for long at room temperature, although it freezes well. It is best to decorate this dessert with fresh fruit just before serving.

## Composition

Tulip base
Passion-fruit mousse
Assorted fresh fruits, such as strawberries and kiwis
Clear glaze

## Recipes

For 50 to 60 servings, 6 cakes, serving 8 to 10 each

## Tulip Batter

6 egg whites
250 g confectioners' sugar (9 oz.)
175 g flour (6 oz.)
125 g butter (4.5 oz.), melted

Mix all the above ingredients together; let the batter rest for 15 minutes. Butter a round sheet pan and spread a thin layer of batter in a circle 2 cm (3/4 in.) in from the edge.

Bake the tulip in a moderate oven at 200°C (375°F) until 2 cm (3/4 in.) of the outer edge becomes golden; it should be white toward the center. Remove the piece from the oven and immediately mold it by turning the tulip into a génoise mold 6 to 8 cm (2.5 to 3 in.) smaller than the tulip. Immediately place a second génoise mold over the tulip to shape it, pressing gently. Be careful not to force it as it becomes firm, as it will easily crack. Unmold the tulip and keep it in a cool, dry place.

**Note:** Individual tulips can be made by spreading a ring of batter 10 to 12 cm (4 to 4.5 in.) in diameter. Again, mold the tulip while it is still hot, immediately after removing it from the oven (if it becomes too cool, it can easily crack during molding). Mold these individual tulips on turned-over glasses or sugar shakers.

## Passion-fruit Mousse

500 ml milk (17 fl. oz.)
500 ml passion-fruit juice (17 fl. oz.)
6 egg yolks
250 g sugar (9 oz.)
80 g flan powder (3 oz.)
8 sheets (16 g) gelatin (1/2 oz.)
500 g Italian meringue (17.5 oz.)
500 ml cream (17 fl. oz.), whipped

## Clear Glaze

To make a clear glaze, bring 500 ml (17 fl. oz.) sugar syrup at 1260 D with 10 g (1/3 oz.) pectin to a boil.

## Assembling the Cake

To prevent the tulip from becoming soggy on the bottom after it is filled, brush a thin layer of barely melted cocoa butter onto the inside of the bottom of the tulip.

Fill the tulip with passion-fruit mousse.

Allow the mousse to set in the refrigerator or freezer.

Just before serving, garnish the top of the mousse with assorted fresh fruits and brush on the clear glaze to finish.

**Note:** The fresh fruits can be replaced with Italian meringue decoratively piped out of a pastry bag and caramelized on top, or Chantilly cream can be used to finish the dessert.

# Orange Kiwi

### Recipes

Serves 35 to 40

### Almond Sponge Cake

8 egg whites, beaten to firm peaks
200 g sugar (7 oz.)
8 egg yolks
150 g cake flour (5 oz.) plus 75 g almond powder (2.5 oz.)

### Orange Mousse

500 ml orange juice (17 fl. oz.)
8 egg yolks
75 g sugar (2.5 oz.)
50 g flan powder (1.5 oz.)
6 sheets (12 g) gelatin (1/2 oz.)
500 g Italian meringue (17.5 oz.)
750 ml cream (25.5 fl. oz.), whipped
75 ml Cointreau (2.5 fl. oz.)

### Cointreau-flavored Sugar Syrup

250 ml sugar syrup (8.5 fl. oz.), at 1260 D
75 ml Cointreau (2.5 fl. oz.)

### Decoration

Slices of kiwi and oranges, 2 to 3 mm (1/16 to 1/8 in.) thick.

### Glaze

Use the clear glaze in Tulipes Passion recipe, page 165.

### Assembling the Cake

Place a cake ring that is 4 to 5 cm (1.5 to 2 in.) high on a cardboard circle or stainless steel sheet pan (a sheet of parchment paper can be placed on the sheet pan).

Place the slices of candied orange and kiwi on the bottom and against the sides of the inside of the ring.

Place a layer of orange mousse in the ring.

Place a thin layer of almond sponge cake moistened with the Cointreau-flavored sugar syrup over the mousse.

Place a second layer of mousse over the sponge cake.

Finish with a second layer of sponge cake moistened with the syrup, which should bring the cake up to the rim of the ring.

Cover with a sheet of plastic wrap and allow the mousse to set in the refrigerator or freezer.

Turn the cake over onto a cardboard circle.

Glaze the top with the clear glaze, using a metal spatula.

Remove the ring by warming the outside.

### Presentation

The orange kiwi cake is fairly easy to make. The cake is constructed upside down and inverted when set. It is a particularly good dessert for warm weather, as it is light and cool.

### Composition

Almond sponge cake
Orange mousse
Slices of kiwi and candied orange
Cointreau-flavored sugar syrup
Clear glaze

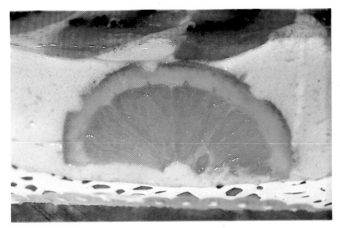
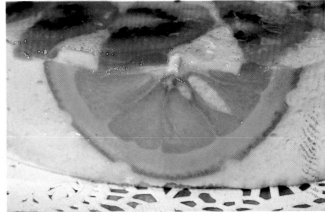

# Mousse mandarine/poire/caramel

### Presentation

The mousse mandarine/poire/caramel cake is fairly easy to make. It is filled with a special mandarin mousse. This cake is particularly interesting because of the combination of flavors: the acidity of the mandarin oranges balanced with the sweetness of the caramelized pears and smoothness of the chocolate ganache.

### Composition

Vanilla/chocolate sponge cake
Chocolate génoise
Mandarin mousse
Pears, quartered and caramelized
Grand Marnier–flavored sugar syrup
Dark-chocolate ganache glaze
Small white-chocolate shavings

### Recipes

Serves 35 to 40

### Vanilla/Chocolate Sponge Cake
For one sheet pan 40 × 60 cm
(16 × 24 in.)

8 egg whites, beaten to firm peaks
200 g sugar (7 oz.)
8 egg yolks
185 g cake flour (6.5 oz.)
15 g cocoa powder (1/2 oz.)
few drops vanilla extract

Whip the egg whites until almost firm peaks form; add the sugar to stiffen them, whisk to firm peaks. Add the egg yolks. Now divide the mixture in half.

Add several drops of vanilla extract to the first half, then fold in 100 g (3.5 oz.) of cake flour.

Fold the remaining cake flour sifted with the cocoa powder into the remaining egg mixture.

Use two pastry bags fitted with no. 7 tips to pipe out diagonal, alternate colors of sponge cake onto a sheet pan covered with buttered parchment paper. Bake the sponge cake.

Cut strips of sponge cake in half lengthwise, so that the two colors are on a bias.

## Chocolate Génoise

For 5 cakes, serving 8 each

16 eggs
500 g sugar (17.5 oz.)
450 g cake flour (16 oz.) plus 50 g cocoa
    powder (1.5 oz.), sifted together

Cut each cake into 1-cm-thick (3/4-in.) layers.

## Mandarin Mousse

500 ml mandarin juice (17 fl. oz.)
8 egg yolks
100 g sugar (3.5 oz.)
50 g flan powder (1.5 oz.)
7 sheets (14 g) gelatin (5 oz.)
500 g Italian meringue (17.5 oz.)
750 ml cream (25.5 fl. oz.), whipped
100 ml Grand Marnier (3.5 fl. oz.)

## Pears, Caramelized and Quartered

1 kg pears (35 oz.) in syrup, drained, cut, and quartered. Sauté in a heavy-bottomed pan with 70 g (2 oz.) sugar until caramelized.

## Grand Marnier–flavored Sugar Syrup

250 ml sugar syrup (8.5 fl. oz.), at 1260 D
50 ml Grand Marnier (1.5 fl. oz.)

## Dark-Chocolate Ganache Glaze

300 ml milk (10 fl. oz.)
300 g semisweet chocolate (10.5 oz.)

Shavings from a piece of white chocolate

### Assembling the Cake

Place a metal cake ring that is 4 to 5 cm (1.5 to 2 in.) high over a cardboard circle and line the inside of the ring with a strip of the vanilla/chocolate-striped sponge cake. Brush on the Grand Marnier–flavored sugar syrup.

Place a disk of chocolate génoise on the bottom of the ring, and brush with the syrup.

Fill the ring halfway with a layer of mandarin mousse.

Garnish the mousse with the caramelized pear quarters.

Place a second layer of chocolate génoise, slightly smaller in diameter than the ring, over the mousse, and brush with the syrup.

Fill with a second layer of mousse just to the rim of the ring, and smooth the top with a metal spatula.

Allow the cake to set in the refrigerator or freezer.

Using a metal spatula, glaze the top of the cake with the dark-chocolate ganache.

Sprinkle white-chocolate shavings on top of the glaze after it has set.

Before serving, remove the cake ring by warming it on the outside.

# 4/21 chocolate/pistachio

## Presentation

4/21, a dice game that has long been popular in French cafés, inspired this cake. This cake is fairly easy to make, contains only a little liquor for those who prefer cakes without a strong liquor flavor, and is cleverly decorated.

## Composition

Almond/chocolate sponge cake
Chocolate whipped cream
Pistachio bavarian
Kirsch-flavored sugar syrup
Chantilly cream and grated coconut, which can be colored pale green (decoration)
Molded chocolate cup and dice made out of marzipan

## Recipes

Serves 30 to 40

### Almond/Chocolate Sponge Cake

8 egg whites
200 g sugar (7 oz.), plus 8 egg yolks
150 g cake flour (5 oz.), plus 50 g almond powder (1.5 oz.), plus 20 g cocoa powder (2/3 oz.), all sifted together

### Chocolate Whipped Cream

1 L heavy cream (34 fl. oz.), whipped
100 g confectioners' sugar (3.5 oz.)
500 g dark chocolate (17.5 oz.), melted

### Pistachio Bavarian

500 ml milk (17 fl. oz.)
200 g sugar (7 oz.)
8 egg yolks
35 g pistachio paste (1 oz.) plus several drops of pistachio extract (green coloring can be added, but is optional)
6 sheets (12 g) gelatin (1/2 oz.)
750 ml heavy cream (25.5 fl. oz.), whipped

### Kirsch-flavored Sugar Syrup

250 ml syrup (8.5 fl. oz.), at 1260 D
25 ml Kirsch (1 fl. oz.), plus several drops vanilla extract

## Assembling the Cake

Place a 4-cm-high (1.5-in.) metal cake ring over a cardboard circle and line it three-quarters of the way up with a strip of almond/chocolate sponge cake. Brush with the Kirsch-flavored sugar syrup.

Place a layer of almond/chocolate sponge cake in the base of the ring and brush it generously with the syrup.

Fill the ring halfway with the chocolate whipped cream.

With a pastry bag and medium-size fluted tip, pipe a border of Chantilly cream on top of the sponge cake. This will serve as a border for the bavarian cream.

Place the cake in a refrigerator or freezer until the cream sets.

Once the cream has set, fill the cake with pistachio bavarian to just below the rim of the Chantilly cream. Allow the cake to set in the refrigerator or freezer. Heat the outside of the metal ring to remove it.

## Decoration

Cover the top of the cake with grated coconut, which can be colored with green coloring (optional).

The chocolate cup can be made with tempered couverture molded in a baba or other similarly shaped mold.

To make the dice, shape cubes of marzipan approximately 1 cm (3/4 in.) square. With a paper cone filled with decorating chocolate, pipe out dots on the dice.

# Ombre et lumière

## Presentation

The ombre et lumière cake is especially appealing to those who like the combination of rum and raisins. This cake is somewhat rich, making it a good dessert for the cooler months. It freezes well and can be quickly decorated as needed.

## Composition

Vanilla sponge cake
Chocolate whipped cream
Rum bavarian
Golden raisins macerated in rum
Rum-flavored sugar syrup
Chocolate shavings (decoration)

## Recipes

Serves 35 to 40

### Vanilla Sponge Cake

10 egg whites
250 g sugar (9 oz.)
250 g cake flour (9 oz.)
several drops vanilla extract
Before baking, the sponge cake can be decorated with melted chocolate piped out of a paper cone.

### Chocolate Whipped Cream

1 L heavy cream (34 fl. oz.), whipped
100 g confectioners' sugar (3.5 oz.)
500 g dark chocolate (17.5 oz.), melted
Gently combine all the above ingredients, mixing gently.

### Rum Bavarian

500 ml milk (17 fl. oz.)
200 g sugar (7 oz.), plus 8 egg yolks
7 sheets (14 g) gelatin (1/2 oz.)
50 ml aged rum (1.5 fl. oz.)
750 ml heavy cream (25.5 fl. oz.), whipped

### Macerated Golden Raisins

300 g golden raisins (10.5 oz.), blanched and macerated for 48 hours in 25 ml aged rum (1 fl. oz.).

### Rum-flavored Sugar Syrup

250 ml sugar syrup (8.5 fl. oz.), at 1260 D
50 ml aged rum (1.5 fl. oz.)

### Decoration

Chocolate shavings made with dark-chocolate couverture

## Assembling the Cake

Place a 4- to 5-cm-high (1.5- to 2-in.) cake ring on a cardboard cake circle and line it to the rim with strips of vanilla sponge cake brushed with rum-flavored sugar syrup. Place a layer of vanilla sponge cake on the bottom inside the ring, and brush it with rum syrup.

Fill the cake halfway with the chocolate whipped cream. Sprinkle the macerated raisins over the cream. Place a second layer of vanilla sponge cake in the ring and brush with rum syrup.

Fill to just below the top of the sponge cake with the rum-flavored bavarian cream. Allow the cake to set in the refrigerator or freezer.

After the cake has set, remove the metal ring without heating the outside. It should come off easily. Decorate the top of the cake with chocolate shavings.

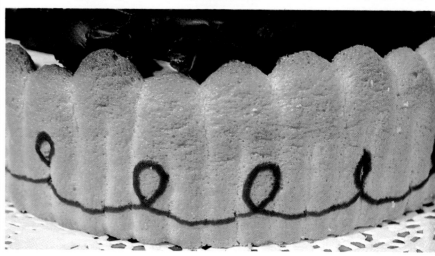

# Le Mogador

## Presentation

In Paris, there is a famous theater, Le Mogador, for which this cake is named. This dessert is very rich and creamy. It is the type of dessert most appreciated by those who are concerned with quality rather than quantity, as small servings are sufficient because of its richness.

Le Mogador can be assembled in bombe molds or long half-moon-shaped molds.

## Composition

Cognac mousse
Macaroons soaked in Cognac-flavored sugar syrup
Italian meringue

## Recipes

Serves 35 to 40

### Cognac Mousse

20 egg yolks
500 ml sugar syrup (8.5 fl. oz.), at 1260 D
12 sheets (24 g) gelatin (3/4 oz.)
1 L heavy cream (34 fl. oz.), whipped
250 g Italian meringue (9 oz.)
100 ml Cognac (3.5 fl. oz.)

### Nancy Macaroons

Use very dry macaroons that can soak up a lot of syrup. Soak them in the Cognac-flavored sugar syrup until they are completely moist.

### Cognac-flavored Sugar Syrup

100 ml sugar syrup (3.5 fl. oz.), at 1260 D
100 ml Cognac (3.5 fl. oz.)

### Assembling the Cake

Fill the mold with Cognac mousse, stopping occasionally to add the Cognac-soaked macaroons so they are evenly dispersed throughout the mousse.

Fill the mold to the rim. Place it in the freezer to set.

Once set, unmold the cake as for ice cream by warming the outside of the mold. Turn the cake onto a cake cardboard or serving platter.

Decorate the cake with Italian meringue, using a pastry bag with a fluted tip; a second pastry bag with a plain tip can be used in addition to or instead of that with the fluted tip. Brown the meringue with a small propane torch.

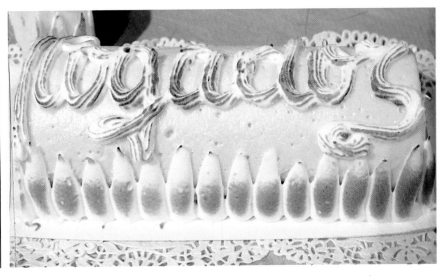

# Modern desserts by Alain Escoffier

## Alain Escoffier

*As co-author of the* Professional French Pastry Series, *Alain Escoffier has already demonstrated his abilities as a versatile and experienced pastry chef.*

*The desserts that follow, Désir Rose, Crépuscule, Stanislas, Caprice aux Pommes, le Petit Bonheur, Miroir Citron/Chocolat, and Charlotte Alliance, further reveal Escoffier's talents as pastry chef. The desserts demonstrate a fine eye for presentation.*

*Being able to create desserts that are as wonderful to eat as they are to look at, and having the ability to apply the many techniques used in pastry making, are the characteristics of a fine pastry chef.*

# Désir rose

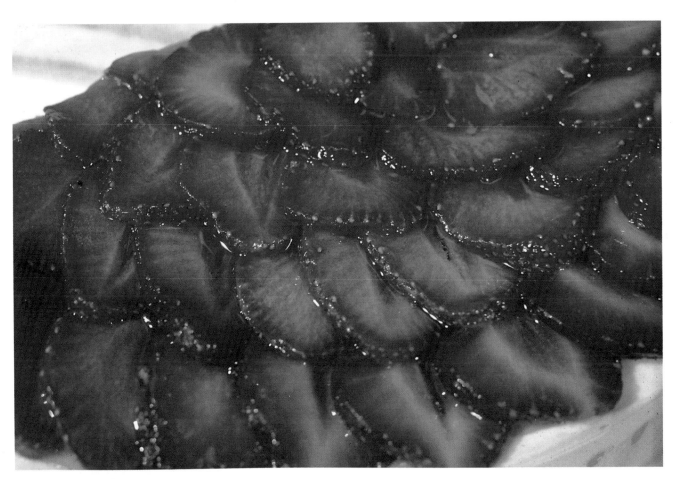

### Presentation

The désir rose is a seasonal dessert served when the best fresh strawberries are available. It is very light, based on fromage blanc, a light fresh cheese with a texture somewhat like creamy yogurt, yet sweeter, without yogurt's tartness.

The strawberries should be placed on the cake just before it is presented. Place the strawberries carefully and neatly, as they serve to decorate the cake.

Without the strawberries, this cake freezes well, so several can be made at once.

### Composition

Strips of ladyfingers
Almond sponge cake or génoise
Vanilla-flavored sugar syrup
Fromage blanc mousse
Strawberries
Strawberry jelly
Ribbon or plastic wrap

### Recipes

Serves 40

### Fromage Blanc Mousse

300 g sugar (10.5 oz.), plus 100 ml water (3.5 fl. oz.), cooked to 120°C (248°F), poured in a fine stream over 6 egg yolks, and whisked until pale
10 sheets (20 g) gelatin (3/4 oz.)
1 kg fromage blanc (35 oz.)
vanilla extract
200 g Italian meringue (7 oz.), optional

### Vanilla-flavored Sugar Syrup

1 L sugar syrup (35 fl. oz.), at 1260 D
20 ml vanilla extract (1/2 fl. oz.)

### Almond Sponge Cake

For 1'sheet pan 40 × 60 cm
(16 × 24 in.)

750 g almond paste (26.5 oz.)
9 eggs
75 g apple compote (2.5 oz.)
100 g cornstarch (3.5 oz.)
150 g butter (5 oz.), melted

#### Preparation

Spread sponge cake batter on a sheet pan and comb it to making vertical lines as a decoration. Bake.

Make a sheet of almond sponge cake or génoise.

#### Assembling the Cake

Place a metal cake ring that is 4 to 4.5 cm (1.5 to 1.75 in.) on a cardboard cake circle.

Line the inside of the cake ring three-quarters of the way up with a strip of ladyfingers.

Place a sheet of almond sponge cake or génoise over the cardboard base and brush generously with vanilla-flavored sugar syrup.

Fill the ring three-quarters of the way up with fromage blanc mousse and cover with a second layer of sponge cake or génoise. Brush with the syrup.

Fill to the rim with fromage blanc mousse and smooth the top with a metal spatula.

Place the cake in the freezer to set.

Once set, remove the metal ring by heating the outside, which can be done with a hot towel.

#### Decorating

Decorate the cake by forming a rosette pattern with slices of strawberries on the top.

Glaze the strawberries with jelly, using a pastry brush.

Place a strip of clear film or a ribbon around the side of the cake.

#### Important!

Place the strawberries on just before serving. The cake itself freezes well, but the strawberries do not and are best served fresh, not frozen.

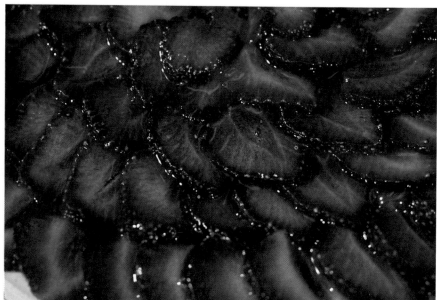

# Le crépuscule

#### Presentation

The crépuscule (sunset) is a very smooth and light cake, making it appropriate for all seasons.

This cake consists of a base of vanilla bavarian covered with an equal amount of chocolate mousse. No liquor is used in this cake.

The crépuscule is easy and quick to prepare, as well as being attractive, though simple to decorate. A sauce such as crème anglaise can accompany the cake when served.

The crépuscule freezes well, enabling the pastry chef to prepare several cakes at a time.

#### Composition

Strips of ladyfingers
Génoise
Vanilla-flavored sugar syrup
Vanilla bavarian
Chocolate mousse
Chocolate shavings
Ribbon

#### Recipes

Serves 40

### Vanilla Bavarian

1 L milk (34 fl. oz.)
400 g sugar (14 oz.)
14 egg yolks
2 vanilla beans
14 sheets (28 g) gelatin (1 oz.)`
1.5 L heavy cream (50.5 fl. oz.), whipped

### Vanilla-flavored Sugar Syrup

1 L sugar syrup (34 fl. oz.), at 1260 D
20 ml vanilla extract (1/2 oz.)

### Chocolate Mousse

20 egg yolks
400 g sugar (14 oz.), plus 100 g glucose
(3.5 oz.), plus 150 ml water (5 fl. oz.),
cooked together to 116°C (240°F)
400 g couverture chocolate (14 oz.),
melted
200 g cocoa powder (7 oz.)
600 g butter (21 oz.), plus 20 ml rum
(1/2 fl. oz.)
400 g sugar (14 oz.), plus 20 ml water
(1/2 fl. oz.), cooked to 120°C (248°F)
500 ml heavy cream (17 fl. oz.)

### Preparation

Make 10-cm-tall (4-in.) strips of ladyfinger piped out with a no. 2 tip.
Make the génoise.

### Assembling the Cake

Place a cake ring that is 4 to 4.5 cm
(1.5 to 1.75 in.) high over a cardboard
circle. Line the inside of the ring with
a strips of ladyfingers cut in half.

Place the génoise over the bottom of
the ring, and brush both the ladyfinger
strip and the génoise with vanilla-
flavored sugar syrup.

Fill the ring halfway with vanilla
bavarian.

Allow the cake to set in the freezer.
Fill with chocolate mousse to the tops
of the ladyfingers, mounding the mousse
slightly higher in the center to form a
dome. Again place the cake in the freezer
to set. Remove the metal ring only after
the cake has set.

### Decoration

Cover the top of the cake with equal
amounts of dark- and milk-couverture-
chocolate shavings.

A ribbon can be placed around the
cake, which enhances its appearance in
displays for window cases in pastry
stores.

# Le Stanislas

### Presentation

The Stanislas is a cake appropriate
throughout the year, as it is very smooth
and light. The base of this cake is made
from savarin dough, which is where it
gets its name, as Stanislas Leszczynski
invented the savarin. This cake is
strongly flavored with liquor, in the same
way as a savarin is.

This cake is easy and quick to assemble and decorate. As it freezes well, it is
possible to prepare several at a time.

## Composition

Chocolate génoise
Savarin
Light sugar syrup at 1115 D
Grand Marnier–flavored sugar syrup at 1260 D
Grand Marnier mousse
Chantilly cream
Sliced, roasted almonds or almond craquelées
Orange sections

## Recipes

Serves 40

### Grand Marnier Mousse

150 g sugar (5 oz.), plus 50 ml water (1.5 fl. oz.), cooked to 120°C (248°F) and poured over 3 egg yolks
1 L heavy cream (34 fl. oz.), plus 150 g confectioners' sugar (5 oz.)
4 sheets (8 g) gelatin (1/4 oz.)
100 ml Grand Marnier (3.5 fl. oz.)

### Grand Marnier–flavored Sugar Syrup

1 L sugar syrup (34 fl. oz.), at 1260 D
150 to 200 ml Grand Marnier (5 to 6.5 fl. oz.)

## Preparation

Bake the savarin dough in génoise molds smaller than the metal cake ring to be used.

Prepare the chocolate génoise and the two syrups. Soak the savarins in the light syrup (this syrup can also be flavored with Grand Marnier if desired).

## Assembling the Cake

Place a metal cake ring that is 4 to 4.5 cm (1.5 to 1.75 in.) high over a cardboard circle.

Place a layer of génoise on the bottom of the ring, and brush it well with Grand Marnier–flavored sugar syrup.

Fill the ring halfway with the Grand Marnier mousse. With a spatula, spread the mousse so that it also lines the ring up to the rim.

Place the moist savarin over the mousse.

Fill the ring with Grand Marnier mousse to just below the rim. Place the cake in the freezer to set.

## Decoration

Spread a layer of Chantilly cream on top of the mousse, up to the top of the the cake, halfway up. Peeled orange sections can be placed on top of the cream if desired.

ring. Decorate the Chantilly cream with a pastry comb or serrated knife.

Place the sliced roasted almonds or almond craquelées around the sides of

## Variation

A ribbon can be placed around the side of the cake and sliced or craquelées almonds can be sprinkled on top.

# Caprice aux poires

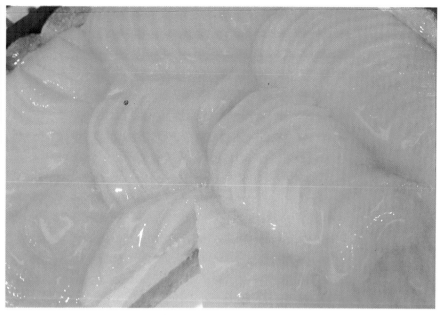

## Presentation

The caprice aux poires cake is particularly light because of the vanilla bavarian or pear mousse that serves as its filling.

This cake is fairly easy and quick to make. Slices of pears are placed on top in a decorative fashion.

As this cake freezes well, it is possible to make several at a time.

## Composition

Ladyfingers
Génoise
Pear-flavored sugar syrup
Vanilla bavarian or pear mousse
Pears in syrup
Pear glaze
Ribbon

## Recipes

Serves 40

## Pear Glaze

1 kg apricot or other golden jelly (35 oz.)
100 ml pear brandy (3.5 fl. oz.)

## Vanilla Bavarian

1 L milk (34 fl. oz.)
12 to 16 egg yolks
400 g sugar (14 oz.)
2 vanilla beans
14 sheets (28 g) gelatin (10 oz.)
1.5 L heavy cream (50.5 fl. oz.), whipped

## Pear-flavored Sugar Syrup

1 L pear juice (34 fl. oz.), plus 750 g of sugar (26.5 oz.), brought to a boil and cooled
200 ml pear brandy (6.5 fl. oz.), added to the pear syrup when it cools

## Preparation

Prepare 10-cm-long (4-in.) ladyfingers, using a no. 12 pastry tip.
Make the génoise.

## Assembling the Cake

Place a metal cake ring that is 4 to 4.5 cm (1.5 to 1.75 in.) high over a cardboard circle.

Line the inside of the ring with a strip of ladyfingers, cut in half lengthwise.

Place a thin layer of génoise inside the ring and brush both the génoise and ladyfingers with pear-flavored sugar syrup.

Fill the cakes with the vanilla bavarian using a ladle. Mound the cream slightly, so that it extends halfway up the ladyfingers but is a bit higher in the center.

Place the cakes in the freezer to set.

## Decoration

Place sliced pear halves decoratively on top of the cake. The pears should be sliced so that the halves are kept together but are slightly flattened, giving the cake a neat and attractive appearance.

Strain the pear glaze, then glaze the pears, using a pastry brush.

Place a ribbon around the outside of the cake.

# Le petit bonheur

## Presentation

The petit bonheur cake is made with fresh seasonal red fruits. It is very smooth and airy, and somewhat easy to make. The cake is brightly decorated with fresh red berries such as red currants or wild strawberries.

As this cake freezes well, it is possible to make several at a time.

## Composition

Ladyfingers
Génoise
Red currant–flavored sugar syrup
Wild strawberry mousse
Red currant mousse
Fresh red currants (garnish)
Red currant jelly
Ribbon

## Recipes

Serves 40

### Wild Strawberry Mousse

500 ml wild strawberry pulp (17 fl. oz.)
8 sheets (16 g) gelatin (1/2 oz.)
750 ml heavy cream (25.5 fl. oz.), whipped
100 g confectioners' sugar (3.5 oz.)

### Red Currant Mousse

500 ml red currant juice or pulp (17 fl. oz.)
10 sheets (20 g) gelatin (3/4 oz.)
750 ml heavy cream (25.5 fl. oz.), whipped
150 g confectioners' sugar (5 oz.)

### Red Currant–flavored Sugar Syrup

350 ml sugar syrup (12 fl. oz.), at 1260 D
500 ml red currant pulp or juice (17 fl. oz.)
350 ml water (12 fl. oz.)
150 ml red currant liqueur (5 fl. oz.)

## Preparation

Prepare the ladyfingers by piping out the ladyfinger batter in strips 10 cm (4 in.) long, using a no. 12 pastry tip.

Make the génoise.

## Assembling the Cake

Place a metal cake ring that is 4 to 4.5 cm (1.5 to 1.75 in.) high over a cardboard circle.

Line the ring with the strips of ladyfinger cut in half lengthwise.

Place a layer of génoise inside the ring. Brush both the ladyfingers and the génoise with red currant syrup. Fill the ring halfway with wild strawberry mousse. Place the cake in the freezer until the mousse is set.

Fill the cake with the red currant mousse, to 5 mm (1/4 in.) from the tops of the ladyfingers, mounding it slightly higher in the center of the cake.

Return the cake to the freezer to set.

## Decoration

Cover the top of the cake with red currants. Brush on a thin layer of clear glaze.

Place a ribbon around the cake.

## Variations

### Petit Bois

Petit bois means little forest, where wild strawberries can be found. The procedure for this cake is the same as for the petit bonheur, except the mousses are reversed so that the wild strawberry mousse is on top. The red currants that cover the cake are replaced with wild strawberries.

### Petit Buisson

To make the petit buisson (little thicket), follow the same procedure as for the petit bois, replacing the wild strawberry mousse with blackberry mousse, using the same recipe as for the wild strawberry mousse. Cover the cake with fresh blackberries instead of wild strawberries. Glaze with blackberry or clear jelly.

### Petit Ardéchois

To make the petit ardéchois, follow the same procedure as for the petit bonheur, replacing either the red currant or wild strawberry mousse with blueberry mousse, made with the same recipe as for the red currant mousse. Cover the cake with blueberries, and brush with a clear glaze.

# Miroir citron/chocolat

## Presentation

All cakes called *miroir* (mirror) are so named because they have a smooth, brilliant glaze on top that almost appears reflective, like a mirror.

The miroir citron/chocolat combines lemon mousse with chocolate génoise over a pistachio-flavored base. No liquor is used in this cake.

This miroir is fairly easy to assemble and stores well in the freezer, making it possible to prepare several cakes at a time.

## Composition

Pistachio sponge cake
Chocolate génoise
Lemon mousse
Lemon-flavored sugar syrup
Lemon glaze
Candied lemon zest

## Recipes

Serves 40

### Lemon-flavored Sugar Syrup

1 L sugar syrup (34 fl. oz.)
100 ml lemon juice (3.5 fl. oz.)

### Pistachio Sponge Cake

For a 40 × 60 cm (16 × 24 in.) sheet pan, which should be covered with parchment paper

750 g almond paste (26.5 oz.) plus 100 g pistachio paste (3.5 oz.) and 9 eggs
75 g apple compote (2.5 oz.)
100 g cornstarch (3.5 oz.)
150 g butter (5 oz.), melted

### Lemon Mousse

500 ml crème fraîche or heavy cream (17 fl. oz.)
12 egg yolks
100 g sugar (3.5 oz.)
50 g flan powder (1.5 oz.)
250 ml lemon juice (8.5 fl. oz.)
9 sheets (18 g) gelatin (1/2 oz.)
20 egg whites, beaten to firm peaks
350 g sugar (12.5 oz.), plus 100 ml water (3.5 fl. oz.), cooked to 120°C (248°F)

### Lemon Glaze

1 kg golden jelly (35 oz.), thinned with 150 ml lemon juice (5 fl. oz.)

### Lemon Zest

Poach a fine julienne of lemon zest in hot sugar syrup, 1260 D, for 1 hour.

## Preparation

Make the pistachio sponge cake.
Make the chocolate génoise.

## Assembling the Cake

Place a metal cake ring that is 4 to 4.5 cm (1.5 to 1.75 in.) high over a cardboard circle. Cut a circular base, from the pistachio sponge cake. Place it over the cardboard, inside the ring.

Fill the ring halfway with lemon mousse.

Place a layer of chocolate génoise that is slightly smaller in diameter than the ring over the mousse. Brush it generously with lemon-flavored sugar syrup.

Fill with lemon mousse just to the rim of the ring. Place the cake in the freezer to set.

## Decoration

Glaze the top of the cake with lemon glaze using a ladle, and smooth it with a metal spatula. Sprinkle candied lemon zest on top of the cake.

Remove the metal ring by heating the outside. Place a thin strip of plastic around the cake to protect it and enhance its presentation.

# Charlotte alliance

### Presentation

The charlotte alliance can be quickly assembled. It is based on a combination of fromage blanc mousse (a very light, fresh cheese) and raspberries. The fresh raspberries that cover the cake make it bright and colorful and particularly appealing to children. No liquor is used in this cake.

The charlotte alliance freezes well, making it possible to prepare several cakes at a time. It is best to freeze this cake without the raspberries on top.

### Composition

Ladyfingers
Génoise
Raspberry-flavored sugar syrup
Fromage blanc mousse
Fresh raspberries
Clear jelly
Ribbon

### Recipes

Serves 40

### Fromage Blanc Mousse

350 g sugar (12.5 oz.), plus 180 g egg yolks (6.5 oz.); prepare as for a bombe batter
1 kg fromage blanc (35 oz.)
18 sheets (36 g) gelatin (1 oz.)

### Raspberry-flavored Sugar Syrup

500 g raspberry pulp (17.5 oz.)
350 ml water (12 fl. oz.)
350 ml sugar syrup (12 fl. oz.), at 1260 D

### Preparation

Make strips of ladyfinger 10 cm (4 in.) long.
Make the génoise.

### Assembling the Cake

Place a metal cake ring that is 4.5 cm (1.75 in.) high over a cardboard circle.
Line the inside of the ring with ladyfingers cut in half.
Place a layer of génoise on the bottom of the ring. Moisten both the génoise and ladyfingers with raspberry-flavored sugar syrup.
Fill the ring with fromage blanc mousse to the tops of the ladyfingers.
Place the cake in the freezer to set.

### Decoration

This cake should be decorated just before serving. Place fresh raspberries on top of the cake and glaze them with a clear jelly, using a pastry brush.
Remove the metal ring, and place a ribbon around the cake.

# Modern desserts by Christian Lejour

## Christian Lejour

The desserts by Christian Lejour on the following pages demonstrate his capabilities and talents as a pastry chef.

Christian Lejour apprenticed in pastry in Burgundy, France. He has worked in several renowned French pastry shops, including Dalloyau and Saffray in Paris.

Lejour has taught pastry in Vincennes, Paris, and is presently an instructor of pastry making at the Centre Technologique Ferrandi in Paris, along with the authors of this series.

Christian Lejour has won numerous medals at various pastry competitions, including the Charles Proust and the Coupe de France.

# Longchamp

## Recipes

Serves 40

### Kirsch Mousse

1 kg pastry cream (35 oz.)
1 L heavy cream (34 fl. oz.), whipped
9 sheets (18 g) gelatin (1/2 oz.)
100 ml Kirsch (3.5 fl. oz.)

### Kirsch-flavored Sugar Syrup

1 L sugar syrup (34 fl. oz.), at 1260 D
150 ml Kirsch (3.5 fl. oz.)

### Preparation

Prepare the ladyfingers by piping them out into strips with a pastry bag and tip or combing a sheet of sponge cake batter spread on a sheet pan. Make the génoise.

### Assembling the Cake

Place a metal ring that is 4.5 cm (1.75 in.) high over a cardboard circle. Line the ring to the rim with strips of ladyfinger or sponge cake.

Place a layer of génoise inside the ring, and brush both the génoise and ladyfingers with Kirsch-flavored sugar syrup.

Fill the cake with Kirsch mousse, sprinkling in raspberries as the cake is filled so the raspberries are well distributed throughout. The cake should be filled to the rim of the ring. Smooth the top of the mousse with a metal spatula.

Freeze the cake until set.

Smooth a thin layer of Italian meringue on top.

### Decoration

Decorate the top of the cake with a pastry bag fitted with a Saint-Honoré tip. Pipe out Italian meringue, from the center, curving outward to the edge of the cake.

Brown the top of the meringue with a small propane torch.

Remove the metal ring and place fresh raspberries in the center of the cake.

## Presentation

The Longchamp is decorated in a simple though original way, with a pinwheel of Italian meringue, which adds a rather elegant touch.

The Longchamp is very light, made of raspberries sprinkled throughout a Kirsch mousse.

This cake is not very difficult to make and freezes well, so several cakes can be prepared at one time.

## Composition

Ladyfingers
Génoise
Raspberries
Kirsch mousse
Italian meringue
Kirsch-flavored sugar syrup

# Rafraîchissant

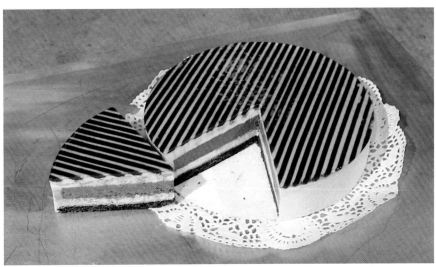

## Presentation

The rafraîchissant cake should be noted for its unusual decoration. The top of the cake is made up of alternate stripes of dark-chocolate ganache and mint-flavored bavarian cream. The mint bavarian makes this cake particularly refreshing, hence its name.

This cake is somewhat tricky to assemble, and requires some experience, as it must be made very neatly. It freezes well, making it possible to prepare several at a time.

## Composition

Chocolate sponge cake
Mint bavarian
Chocolate mousse
Glaze (pale green)
Ganache
Gold ribbon

## Recipes

Serves 40

## Mint Bavarian

500 ml milk (17 fl. oz.)
25 g mint leaves (1 oz.)

10 egg yolks
125 g sugar (4.5 oz.)
90 g powdered gelatin (3 oz.)
1 L heavy cream (34 fl. oz.), whipped

## Chocolate Mousse

500 ml milk (17 fl. oz.)
150 g egg yolks (5 oz.)
175 g sugar (6 oz.)
500 g chocolate (17.5 oz.)
1 L heavy cream (34 fl. oz.)

## Chocolate Sponge Cake

For 1 sheet pan, 40 × 60 (16 × 24 in.)

750 g almond paste (26.5 oz.)
9 eggs
30 g apple compote (1 oz.)
100 g cornstarch (3.5 oz.)
50 g cocoa powder (1.5 oz.)
150 g butter (5 oz.), melted

## Preparation

Prepare the chocolate sponge cake.
One day ahead (or more), mold the chocolate mousse in a ring slightly smaller than the diameter of the ring to be used to mold the cake. Freeze until ready to use.

Place a layer of ganache on a sheet of plastic or plastic wrap and very carefully run a pastry comb through it while it is semiliquid to make strips. Place it in the freezer to set.

## Assembling the Cake

This cake is assembled inversely and turned over when finished. Set the combed ganache on a cardboard circle. Place a 4.5-cm-high (1.75-in.) metal cake ring over the sheet of combed ganache.
Fill the ring halfway with mint bavarian.
Place the frozen chocolate mousse in the center of the ring.
Fill the ring with mint bavarian until it is three-quarters full.
Place a layer of chocolate sponge cake on top.
Freeze the cake until set.
Turn the cake over, place it on a cardboard disk, and remove the plastic film and cardboard from the top.

## Decoration

Glaze the cake.
Remove the ring and place a sheet of gold cardboard or ribbon around the side of the cake.

# Chantilly

### Presentation

The Chantilly is a somewhat seasonal cake, best made when a variety of fresh fruit is available. The bright colors of the fruit make this cake especially attractive in a display, either on a dessert cart or in the window of a pastry shop.

This cake should be garnished with fresh fruit just before it is to be served or displayed. Without fruit, this cake freezes well, making it possible to prepare several at a time and decorate them as needed. No liquor is used in this cake.

### Composition

Sweetened tart dough (pâte sucrée)
Crushed raspberries
Fromage blanc mousse
Chantilly cream
Chocolate sprinkles
Assorted fruit, such as strawberries, raspberries, kiwis, bananas, apricots, cherries, oranges, peaches, pears, red currants, grapes, and melon

### Recipe

#### Fromage Blanc Mousse

Prepare the following as for a bombe batter:
350 g sugar (12.5 oz.) plus 100 ml water (3.5 fl. oz.), cooked to 125°C (257°F) and added to 180 g egg yolks (6.5 oz.)
1 kg fromage blanc (35 oz.)
18 sheets (36 g) gelatin (1.2 oz.)
1 L heavy cream (34 fl. oz.), whipped

### Preparation

Mold the fromage blanc mousse in a savarin mold; various sizes of molds can be used. Place the molded mousse in the freezer until completely frozen.

Roll out the sweetened tart dough 3 mm (1/8 in.) thick and cut to the size of the savarin mold used. Bake the dough.

Unmold the mousse.

### Assembling the Cake

Spread a thin layer of crushed raspberries over the layer of baked sweetened tart dough.

Place the frozen mousse over the dough. Brush a layer of crushed raspberries over the mousse if desired.

Cover the mousse with a thin layer of Chantilly cream.

Using a Saint-Honoré tip, decoratively pipe out Chantilly cream from the center of the cake (do not cover the middle where the fruit will be placed), curving outward to the edge.

Smooth the sides of the cake and decorate the bottom of the sides with chocolate sprinkles.

Garnish the center with fresh fruit.

Brush the fruit with a clear glaze, using a pastry brush.

# L'Antillais

## Presentation

The Antillais cake combines chocolate and banana. This dessert is fairly simple to assemble, although somewhat time consuming. It freezes well, and so it is practical to make several at a time and freeze them.

The cake can be decorated simply with a rosette of kiwis and bananas or more elegantly with tempered chocolate and bananas. It is best to decorate this cake to order.

## Composition

Chocolate sponge cake
Almond meringue
Rum-flavored sugar syrup at 1260 D
Banana slices
Chocolate bavarian
Clear jelly glaze
Banana slices, kiwis, chocolate couverture (decoration)
Gold ribbon

### Recipes

**Chocolate Bavarian**

1 L milk (34 fl. oz.)
300 g egg yolks (10.5 oz.)
350 g sugar (12.5 oz.)

1 kg chocolate (35 oz.)
2 L heavy cream (67.5 fl. oz.), whipped

**Almond Meringue**

750 g egg whites (26.5 oz.)
750 g tant pour tant (equal parts almond powder and sugar) (26.5 oz.)
200 g confectioners' sugar (7 oz.)
600 g granulated sugar (21 oz.)
50 g cornstarch (1.5 oz.)
150 ml milk (5 fl. oz.)

**Chocolate Sponge Cake**

For 40 × 60 cm (16 × 24 in.) sheet pan. Bake at 250°C (475°F).

750 g almond paste (26.5 oz.)
9 eggs
75 g apple compote (2.5 oz.)
50 g cocoa powder (1.5 oz.)
100 g cornstarch (3.5 oz.)
150 g butter (5 oz.), melted

### Preparation

Make the chocolate sponge cake and almond meringue.

Sauté six to eight sliced bananas in butter (with lemon juice to prevent them from browning) and flambé with rum.

### Assembling the Cake

Use a 4.5-cm-high (1.75-in.) metal cake ring to assemble the cake. Cut a layer of sponge cake with the metal ring and place it inside the ring, over a cardboard circle. Generously brush with rum-flavored sugar syrup.

Fill the ring three-quarters full with chocolate bavarian. Place a layer of bananas over the bavarian. Cover the bananas with a layer of almond meringue (a layer of bavarian can cover the bananas before adding the meringue if desired).

Fill the ring to the rim with chocolate bavarian and smooth the top with a metal spatula.

Place the cake in the freezer. Remove the metal ring after the cake is frozen.

### Decoration

The cake can be decorated with slices of kiwis and bananas or strips of tempered chocolate couverture, as shown in the photographs. Brush the fruit with clear glaze and place a gold ribbon or cardboard band around the side of the cake.

# Prestige passion framboise

## Presentation

The prestige passion framboise can be made year-round, as fresh or frozen raspberries can be used for this cake.

The cake is based on a passion-fruit mousse and highlighted with raspberry-flavored sugar syrup and raspberry glaze, which gives it a very festive appearance.

This cake freezes well, making it possible to prepare several at a time. It is quite simple to assemble.

## Composition

Pistachio sponge cake
Génoise
Passion-fruit mousse
Raspberry-flavored sugar syrup
Raspberry glaze
Fresh or frozen raspberries

## Recipes

### Pistachio Sponge Cake

For two 40 × 60 cm (16 × 24 in.) sheet pans

750 g almond paste (26.5 oz.)
100 g pistachio paste (3.5 oz.)
9 eggs

75 g apple compote (2.5 oz.)
100 g cornstarch (3.5 oz.)
150 g butter (5 oz.), melted

### Passion-fruit Mousse

1 kg passion-fruit mousse (35 oz.)
16 to 18 sheets (32 to 36 g) gelatin (approximately 1 oz.)
1.5 L heavy cream (50.5 fl. oz.), whipped
300 g confectioners' sugar (10.5 oz.)
juice of one lemon

### Raspberry Glaze

500 g raspberry pulp (17.5 oz.)
500 g sugar (17.5 oz.)
50 g glucose (1.5 oz.)
40 g pectin (1.5 oz.)

### Raspberry-flavored Sugar Syrup

500 g raspberry pulp (17.5 oz.)
350 ml water (12 fl. oz.)
350 ml sugar syrup (12 fl. oz.), at 1260 D
150 ml raspberry liqueur (5 fl. oz.)

## Preparation

Make the pistachio sponge cake. When the sponge cake is done, layer strips of it with raspberry preserves. This will be used to decorate the sides of the cake.

## Assembling the Cake

Place a metal cake ring that is 4.5 cm (1.75 in.) high over a cardboard circle.

Line the ring with cut strips of the layered sponge cake and preserves.

Place a thin layer of génoise inside the ring, and brush both the sponge cake and the génoise generously with raspberry-flavored sugar syrup.

Fill the ring to the rim with passion-fruit mousse and smooth the top with a metal spatula.

Place the cake in the freezer to set.

Glaze the cake when needed with the raspberry glaze, using a ladle. Quickly smooth the glaze with a metal spatula before it sets.

Remove the metal ring.

Decorate the cake with fresh raspberries if available (frozen raspberries can be substituted).

Place a plastic strip around the side of the cake to prevent it from drying out.

# Perlia

## Presentation

The perlia (pearl) is a very light and creamy cake. A layer of light coffee mousse is combined with a smooth layer of caramel bavarian. The perlia is topped with a thin layer of shiny caramel glaze, from which it gets its name.

The perlia is fairly simple and quick to make and freezes well, making it possible to prepare several cakes at a time.

## Composition

Ladyfingers
Coffee mousse
Caramel bavarian
Coffee génoise
Coffee/rum-flavored sugar syrup
Caramel glaze
Walnuts

## Recipes

Serves 40

### Caramel Bavarian

1 L milk (34 fl. oz.)
16 eggs
500 g caramel (17.5 oz.)
16 sheets (32 g) gelatin (1 oz.)
1.5 L cream (50.5 fl. oz.)

### Coffee Mousse

500 ml milk (17 fl. oz.)
150 g sugar (5 oz.) - 8 egg yolks
25 g instant coffee granules (1.5 Tbsp.)
80 g powdered gelatin (3 oz.)
400 g Italian meringue (14 oz.)
500 ml heavy cream (17 fl. oz.), whipped
50 ml rum (1.5 fl. oz.)

### Coffee Génoise

16 eggs - 500 g sugar (17.5 oz.)
20 g instant coffee granules (1.5 Tbsp.)
500 g cake flour (17.5 oz.)

### Caramel Glaze

1 kg apricot or clear jelly (35 oz.)
200 g caramel (7 oz.)

### Coffee/Rum-flavored Sugar Syrup

1 L sugar syrup (34 fl. oz.), at 1260 D
100 ml water (3.5 fl. oz.), brought to a boil and mixed with 15 g instant coffee granules (1/2 oz.)
50 ml rum (1.5 fl. oz.), added to coffee when cool

## Preparation

Make the ladyfingers by either piping out the batter using a no. 7 pastry tip or spreading the batter on parchment paper and combing it to create decorative vertical lines. Make the génoise.

## Assembling the Cake

Place a 4.5-cm-high (1.75-in.) metal cake ring over a cardboard circle and line it with strips of ladyfinger 3 cm (1.25 in.) high. Place a thin layer of génoise inside the ring, and brush both the génoise and ladyfingers with coffee/rum-flavored sugar syrup.

Fill the ring to the tops of the ladyfingers with caramel bavarian. Sprinkle chopped walnuts over the cream if desired.

Fill the cake to the rim of the ring with coffee mousse, and smooth the top with a metal spatula.

## Decoration

Glaze the top of the cake with the caramel glaze and place a few walnuts decoratively in the center of the cake. Remove the cake ring.

# Délice poire caramel

8 to 10 sheets (16 to 20 g) gelatin (1/2 to 2/3 oz.)
750 ml heavy cream (25.5 fl. oz.), whipped
100 g Italian meringue (3.5 oz.)
50 ml pear brandy (1.5 fl. oz.)

## Caramel Bavarian

500 ml milk (17 fl. oz.)
8 to 10 egg yolks
250 g caramel (9 oz.)
8 sheets (16 g) gelatin (1/2 oz.)
750 ml heavy cream (25.5 fl. oz.), whipped

## Pear-flavored Sugar Syrup

500 ml pear juice (17 fl. oz.) plus 375 g sugar (13 oz.), brought to a boil and cooled
100 ml pear brandy (3.5 fl. oz.), added to syrup when cool

### Preparation

Make ladyfingers flavored with coffee extract.

Make the génoise. Poach the pears.

### Assembling the cake

Place a 4.5-cm-high (1.75-in.) metal cake ring on a cardboard circle and line the inside of the ring with strips of coffee ladyfingers.

Place a thin layer of génoise inside the ring and brush both the ladyfingers and génoise with pear-flavored sugar syrup.

Fill the ring with caramel bavarian almost to the tops of the ladyfingers. If desired, scatter poached pear slices over the caramel bavarian.

Place the cake in the freezer until set.

Fill to the rim of the ring with pear bavarian.

Smooth the top of the cake with a metal spatula, and place it in the freezer until set.

### Presentation

The délice poire caramel is imaginatively decorated with a marble glaze. The cake brings together the flavors of pear and caramel: two layers of bavarian cream, pear and caramel, are separated by a layer of poached pears.

This cake is fairly easy to make and freezes well, so several cakes can be prepared at one time.

### Composition

Coffee ladyfingers
Génoise
Pear bavarian
Caramel bavarian
Pear-flavored sugar syrup
Apricot glaze
Pear slices

### Recipes

Serves 40

### Pear Bavarian

500 ml pear pulp (17 fl. oz.)
8 to 10 egg yolks
25 g sugar (1.5 Tbsp.)

### Decoration

Warm and strain the apricot glaze. Mix in a few drops of coffee extract, stirring only enough to achieve a marble effect; do not stir too much. Glaze the cake with a ladle and smooth the glaze with a metal spatula. Remove the cake ring when the glaze is set.

# Cardinal cassis

## Presentation

The cardinal cassis can be made throughout the year, as frozen black currant puree can be used when fresh currants are not available. This cake is decorated with a black currant glaze and chocolate shavings, which make this cake very elegant looking.

This cake is fairly simple to make, and it freezes well, making it possible to prepare several cakes at one time.

## Composition

Almond meringue
Génoise
Black currant mousse
Black currant–flavored sugar syrup
Black currant glaze
Chocolate shavings

## Recipes

Serves 40

## Black Currant Mousse

1 kg black currant pulp (35 oz.)
16 to 20 sheets (32 to 40 g) gelatin (1 to 1.5 oz.)
1.5 L cream (50.5 fl. oz.), whipped with 300 g sugar (10.5 oz.)
juice of one lemon

## Black Currant–flavored Sugar Syrup

500 g black currant pulp (17.5 oz.)
400 ml water (13.5 fl. oz.)
100 ml sugar syrup (3.5 fl. oz.), at 1260 D
150 ml black currant liqueur (5 fl. oz.)

## Black Currant Glaze

500 g black currant pulp (17.5 oz.)
500 g sugar (17.5 oz.)
50 g glucose (1.5 oz.)
40 g pectin (1.5 oz.)

## Almond Meringue

750 g egg whites (26.5 oz.), beaten to firm peaks
750 g tant pour tant (equal parts sugar and almond powder) (26.5 oz.)
200 g confectioners' sugar (7 oz.)
600 g granulated sugar (21 oz.)
50 g cornstarch (1.5 oz.)
150 ml milk (5 fl. oz.)

## Preparation

Make the almond meringue and génoise.

## Assembling the Cake

Place a 4.5-cm-high (1.75-in.) metal cake ring over a cardboard circle.

Inside the ring, place a layer of almond meringue cut slightly smaller in diameter than the ring.

Fill the ring halfway with black currant mousse.

Place a layer of génoise, slightly smaller in diameter than the ring, over the mousse, and brush the génoise with black currant–flavored sugar syrup.

Fill the ring to the rim with black currant mousse.

Place the cake in the freezer until frozen.

## Decoration

Glaze the cake with black currant glaze with a ladle, and smooth with a metal spatula.

Remove the cake ring. Gently press chocolate shavings around the sides of the cake.

# Modern desserts by Bernard Respaut

## Bernard Respaut

*Bernard Respaut has an impressive list of training and professional credentials. After an apprenticeship in pastry making, he worked in renowned pastry shops throughout France, fulfilling what is called the Tour de France, working for and training with some of finest pastry chefs in France. He then received the Brevet de Maitrise, a diploma in pastry making.*

*Bernard Respaut has worked as pastry making instructor at the school CFA in Vincennes, Paris, before joining the Centre Technologique Ferrandi and becoming a colleague of the authors of this series.*

*Respaut has won many competitions in France, including the Charles Proust, Coupe de France, and Cedus awards, as well as international competitions.*

*The desserts made by Bernard Respaut cover a wide range of pastry making, using a variety of doughs and batters, mousses and creams and a variety of flavors and original decorations.*

# Rêve des îles

## Presentation

The rêve des îles (dream island) combines the flavors of rum and chocolate, with raisins sprinkled throughout. It is simply and beautifully decorated with an orchid and leaves made from pulled sugar.

## Composition

Chocolatine cream
Rum bavarian
Chocolate sponge cake
Raisins macerated in rum
Sugar syrup at 1260 D

## Recipes

Serves 20 to 25

### Chocolate Sponge Cake

24 egg yolks
12 eggs
350 g sugar (12.5 oz.)
250 g cake flour (9 oz.)
150 g cocoa powder (5 oz.)
10 g baking powder (2 tsp.)

### Chocolatine Cream

500 g chocolate ganache (17.5 oz.)
250 g pastry cream (9 oz.)
1 L heavy cream (34 fl. oz.), whipped
25 ml rum (1 fl. oz.)

### Rum Bavarian

500 ml milk (17 fl. oz.)
180 g sugar (6.5 oz.)
160 g (8) egg yolks (5.5 oz.)
32 g gelatin (1 oz.)
25 ml rum (1 fl. oz.)
500 ml heavy cream (17 fl. oz.), whipped

### Rum-flavored Sugar Syrup

200 ml sugar syrup (6.5 fl. oz.), at 1260 D
50 ml aged rum (1.5 fl. oz.)

### Assembling the Cake

Place a metal cake ring that is 3 to 4 cm (1.25 to 1.5 in.) high over a card-

board circle.

Place a layer of chocolate sponge cake that has a smaller diameter than the ring inside the ring. Brush generously with the rum-flavored sugar syrup, and sprinkle with 200 g (7 oz.) rum-macerated raisins.

Line the ring with the chocolatine cream. Fill the ring half full with rum bavarian.

Fill to the rim with chocolatine cream.
Place the cake in the freezer until frozen. Remove the ring by warming it, and return the cake to the freezer.

### Decoration

Spray the cake with chocolate using a spray gun to create a velvet texture.
Place an orchid and leaves made from pulled sugar in the center of the cake.

# Irish coffee

### Coffee Bavarian

400 ml milk (13.5 fl. oz.)
50 g coffee beans (1.5 oz.), ground very
  coarsely
6 egg yolks
140 g sugar (5 oz.)
20 g instant coffee granules (1/2 oz.)
16 g gelatin (1/2 oz.)
1 L heavy cream (34 fl. oz.), whipped
whiskey, to taste

### Light Coffee Cream

750 g butter (26.5 oz.)
750 g Italian meringue (26.5 oz.)
70 ml coffee extract (2.5 fl. oz.)
50 ml whiskey (1.5 fl. oz.)

### Whiskey-flavored Sugar Syrup

250 ml sugar syrup (8.5 fl. oz.), at
  1260 D
75 ml whiskey (2.5 fl. oz.)

### Assembling the Cake

Place a metal cake ring that is 3 to
4 cm (1.25 to 1.5 in.) over a cardboard
circle.
Line the inside of the ring three-
quarters high with coffee génoise if desired. Place a thin layer of coffee génoise
over the bottom of the cardboard, and
generously brush the sides and base with
whiskey-flavored sugar syrup.
Fill the ring one-third full with light
coffee cream. Place a second thin layer
of coffee génoise on top and brush it
with whiskey syrup.
Fill the cake to the rim with coffee
bavarian. Place the cake in the freezer.
When the cake is frozen, remove the
metal cake ring by warming it with a
hot towel or small propane torch.
Cover the top of the cake with a
thin layer of coffee-flavored marzipan or
fondant.

### Decoration

Place a strip of decoratively cut tempered couverture chocolate around the
side of the cake. Spray coffee extract
with an airbrush to create light to dark
stripes on top of the marzipan or fondant.

### Presentation

The Irish coffee cake blends the flavors
of coffee and whiskey, like the drink of
the same name. This cake can be made
throughout the year and has a relatively
low food cost.

### Composition

Coffee génoise
Coffee bavarian
Light coffee cream
Whiskey-flavored sugar syrup

### Recipes

Serves 25 to 30

### Coffee Génoise

800 g eggs (28 oz.)
500 g sugar (17.5 oz.)
500 g cake flour (17.5 oz.)
200 g butter (7 oz.)
20 ml coffee extract (4 tsp.)

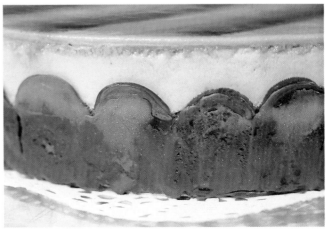

# Le rucher

## Presentation

A rucher, or apiary, is a beehouse containing a number of beehives. This cake is based on a combination of honey bavarian, honey meringue, and raspberry mousse. The optional decoration with langues-de-chat (cat's tongue cookies) wrapped around the side of the cake is fairly simple to make.

## Composition

Honey sponge cake
Raspberry mousse
Honey bavarian
Honey meringue
Italian meringue
Honey/raspberry glaze
White wine/honey–flavored sugar syrup
Langues-de-chat

## Recipes

Serves 30

### Honey Sponge Cake

18 egg yolks
150 g sugar (5 oz.)
150 g honey (5 oz.)
300 g butter (10.5 oz.), melted
200 g cake flour (7 oz.)
200 g almond paste (7 oz.)

### Raspberry Mousse

500 g raspberry (17.5 oz.)
150 g sugar (5 oz.)
12 g gelatin (1/2 oz.)
500 ml heavy cream (17 fl. oz.), whipped
150 g Italian meringue (5 oz.)

### Honey Bavarian

100 g honey (3.5 oz.)
12 egg yolks
200 ml white wine (6.5 fl. oz.)
16 g gelatin (1/2 oz.)

### Honey Meringue

600 g honey (21 oz.), plus 200 ml water (6.5 fl. oz.), cooked to 115°C (239°F)
8 egg whites, beaten to firm peaks
300 ml heavy cream (10 fl. oz.)

### White Wine/Honey–flavored Sugar Syrup

5 ml white wine (1 tsp.)
95 ml sugar syrup (3 fl. oz.), at 1260 D
50 ml mead (1.5 fl. oz.), or other honey liquor

## Assembling the Cake

Place a metal cake ring that is 3 to 4 cm (1.25 to 1.5 in.) high over a cardboard circle.

Line the inside of the ring with langues-de-chat. Place a layer of honey sponge cake inside the ring and brush it with white wine–flavored sugar syrup.

Place a layer of raspberry mousse over the sponge cake. Add a second layer of sponge cake over the mousse and brush with syrup.

Place a layer of honey bavarian over the sponge cake. Cover with a third layer of sponge cake and brush with syrup.

Add a second layer of raspberry mousse and place the cake in the freezer.

When the cake is frozen, add a final layer of honey bavarian, then smooth over a thin layer of raspberry mousse. (As shown in the photos, the layers of bavarian and mousse may be reversed if desired.) Return the cake to the freezer until set.

## Decoration

Remove the cake ring, and cover the top of the cake with honey/raspberry glaze.

Using a pastry bag fitted with a no. 5 tip, pipe out a crisscross pattern of Italian meringue over the top of the cake. Brown the meringue lightly with a small propane torch.

# Le Sicilien

## Presentation

The Sicilien can be made year-round and has a relatively low food cost. It is a light and airy cake based on a combination of pistachio mousse and pear bavarian.

## Composition

Pistachio macaroon
Pistachio mousse
Pear bavarian
Nut brittle
Pistachio/pear-flavored sugar syrup

## Recipes

Serves 30

## Pistachio Macaroon

400 g almond paste (14 oz.)
75 g pistachio paste (2.5 oz.)
300 g confectioners' sugar (10.5 oz.)
120 ml milk (4 fl. oz)
16 egg whites, beaten to stiff peaks
300 g sugar (10.5 oz.)

## Pear Bavarian

500 g pears (17.5 oz.)
250 ml milk (8.5 fl. oz.)
150 g sugar (5 oz.)
6 egg yolks
20 g gelatin (1/2 oz.)
500 ml heavy cream (17 fl. oz.), whipped
50 ml pear brandy (1.5 fl. oz.)

## Pistachio Mousse

500 ml milk (17 fl. oz.)
250 g sugar (9 oz.)
8 egg yolks
100 g pistachio paste (3.5 oz.)
14 g gelatin (1/2 oz.)
500 ml cream (17 fl. oz.), whipped, plus pistachio liqueur to flavor

## Assembling the Cake

Place a metal cake ring that is 3 to 4 cm (1.25 to 1.5 in.) high over a cardboard circle.

Place a layer of pistachio macaroon inside the ring, and brush it with sugar syrup at 1260 D that has been flavored with pear liqueur and pistachio extract.

Fill the ring one-third full with the pistachio mousse.

Cover the pistachio mousse with a layer of pistachio macaroon slightly smaller than the diameter of the ring, and brush it with pistachio/pear-flavored sugar syrup.

Add a layer of pear bavarian and cover with a layer of pistachio macaroon. Brush with the syrup.

Fill the ring to the rim with pistachio mousse and place the cake in the freezer to set.

Remove the cake ring by warming the outside with a small propane torch.

## Decoration

Cover the top and sides of the cake with almond brittle.

Place roses and leaves made from pulled sugar on top of the cake.

# São Paulo

## Presentation

The São Paulo cake combines the flavors of coffee and chocolate by including a mousse of each flavor. It is decorated with large chocolate shavings that cover the entire cake. As this cake is somewhat rich, it is usually served during the winter months.

## Composition

Coffee sponge cake
Chocolate sponge cake
Chocolate mousse
Coffee mousse
Cognac-flavored sugar syrup

## Recipes

Serves 25 to 30

### Chocolate Sponge Cake

24 egg yolks
12 eggs
350 g sugar (12.5 oz.)
250 g cake flour (9 oz.)
150 g cocoa powder (5 oz.)
10 g baking powder (2 tsp.)

### Coffee Sponge Cake

10 egg yolks
10 egg whites, beaten to firm peaks
250 g sugar (9 oz.)
250 g cake flour (9 oz.)
60 ml coffee extract (2 fl. oz.)

### Coffee Mousse

400 ml milk (14 fl. oz.)
50 g coffee beans (1.5 oz.), coarsely ground
6 egg yolks
140 g sugar (5 oz.)
20 g instant coffee granules (1.5 Tbsp.)
12 g gelatin (1/2 oz.)
200 g Italian meringue (7 oz.)
1 L heavy cream (34 fl. oz.), whipped
100 ml coffee extract (3.5 fl. oz.)

### Chocolate Mousse

Bombe Mixture
16 egg yolks plus 200 g sugar (7 oz.)
200 ml water (6.5 fl. oz.) plus 200 g cocoa powder (7 oz.)
350 g semisweet chocolate (12.5 oz.), melted - 300 g butter (10.5 oz.), melted
100 ml Cognac (3.5 fl. oz.)
16 egg whites, whipped to firm peaks and made into Italian meringue with 500 g sugar (17.5 oz.) cooked to 118°C (244°F)

### Cognac-flavored Sugar Syrup

350 ml sugar syrup (12 fl. oz.), at 1260 D
150 ml Cognac (5 fl. oz.)

### Assembling the Cake

Place a metal cake ring that is 3 to 4 cm (1.25 to 1.5 in.) high over a cardboard circle.

Line the inside of the ring three-quarters high with coffee sponge cake. Place a layer of chocolate sponge cake on the bottom of the ring. Brush the sponge cake on the sides and bottom with Cognac-flavored sugar syrup.

Fill the ring one-third full with coffee mousse, and place a layer of chocolate sponge cake over it. Brush the sponge cake with Cognac-flavored sugar syrup.

Fill the ring to the rim with chocolate mousse.

Place the cake in the freezer.

When the cake is set, remove the ring by warming the outside with a small propane torch.

### Decoration

Decorate the cake with tempered couverture chocolate. Make large shavings to cover the top of the cake and small rectangles to cover the sides. The rectangles can be attached to the sides with chocolate mousse.

# Black is weett

## Dark-Chocolate Mousse

500 g chocolate (17.5 oz.)
100 g unsweetened chocolate (3.5 oz.)
10 egg yolks
50 g confectioners' sugar (1.5 oz.)
16 egg whites, beaten to firm peaks
500 ml heavy cream (17 fl. oz.)
200 g butter (7 oz.), melted

## White-Chocolate Mousse

500 g white chocolate (17.5 oz.)
200 g butter (7 oz.), melted
16 egg whites, beaten to firm peaks
400 ml heavy cream (13.5 fl. oz.)

## Vanilla-flavored Sugar Syrup

350 ml sugar syrup (12 fl. oz.), at
  1260 D, made with 2 vanilla beans

## Assembling the Cake

Place a metal cake ring that is 4 cm
(1.5 in.) high over a cardboard circle.

Line the ring with vanilla sponge cake.
Place a layer of vanilla sponge cake that
is 2.5 cm (1 in.) smaller in diameter than
the ring on the bottom. Brush the sponge
cake on the bottom and sides with
vanilla-flavored sugar syrup.

Fill the ring with a layer of dark-
chocolate mousse. Cover the mousse with
a layer of chocolate sponge cake and
brush with vanilla-flavored sugar syrup.

Fill the ring to the rim with a layer of
dark-chocolate mousse.

Add a layer of white-chocolate mousse,
and cover with a layer of vanilla sponge
cake that has been soaked in vanilla-
flavored sugar syrup.

## Presentation

This is a rich dessert that is best served
during the colder months. The cake is
based on a white-chocolate mousse and
a dark-chocolate mousse held together
with sponge cake.

## Composition

Chocolate and vanilla sponge cakes
Dark-chocolate mousse
White-chocolate mousse
Vanilla-flavored sugar syrup

## Recipes

Serves 25

## Chocolate Sponge Cake

10 egg yolks
250 g sugar (9 oz.)
200 g cake flour (7 oz.)
50 g cocoa powder (1.5 oz.)
10 egg whites, beaten to firm peaks

## Decoration

Decorate the top of the cake by alter-
nately piping out white- and dark-
chocolate mousse using a pastry bag fitted with a large plain tip.

The sponge cake around the side of
the cake can be replaced with a band of
tempered dark chocolate that is attached
to the cake after it is assembled.

# Cœur fidèle

## Presentation

The cœur fidèle (faithful heart) is based on a combination of chestnut bavarian and praline (hazelnut) mousseline. Both flavors originated in the Ardèche region in southern France. A progrès meringue made with hazelnuts and almonds is used as the base.

## Composition

Almond sponge cake
Progrès meringue
Chestnut bavarian
Praline mousseline cream
Rum-flavored sugar syrup

## Recipes

Serves 25

### Almond Sponge Cake

10 egg yolks
10 egg whites
250 g sugar (9 oz.)
200 g cake flour (7 oz.)
50 g almond powder (1.5 oz.)
50 g butter (1.5 oz.), melted
vanilla extract or bean

### Rum-flavored Sugar Syrup

350 ml sugar syrup (12 fl. oz.), at 1260 D
150 ml rum (5 fl. oz.)

### Progrès Meringue

16 egg whites
500 g sugar (17.5 oz.)
250 g almond powder (9 oz.)
250 g hazelnut powder (9 oz.)

### Praline Mousseline Cream

500 ml milk (17 fl. oz.)
125 g sugar (4.5 oz.)
6 egg yolks
60 g cornstarch (2 oz.)
250 g butter (9 oz.)
250 g praline paste (9 oz.)

### Chestnut Bavarian

250 ml milk (8.5 fl. oz.)
150 g sugar (5 oz.)

6 egg yolks
8 sheets (16 g) gelatin (5 oz.)
450 g chestnut puree (16 oz.)
500 ml heavy cream (17 fl. oz.), whipped

## Assembling the Cake

Place a metal cake ring that is 3.5 to 4 cm (1.4 to 1.5 in.) high over a cardboard circle.

Line the inside of the ring halfway up with the almond sponge cake, and brush it with rum-flavored sugar syrup.

Place a layer of progrès inside the ring, and brush it with rum-flavored sugar syrup.

Place a layer of praline mousseline cream over the progrès, cover it with a layer of almond sponge cake, and brush the sponge cake with rum syrup.

Fill the cake almost to the rim with chestnut bavarian and cover it with almond sponge cake. Generously brush the sponge cake with rum syrup.

Spread a layer of chestnut bavarian over the sponge cake, to the rim of the ring.

Place the cake in the freezer until set.

Remove the ring by heating it with a small propane torch.

## Decoration

Cover the top of the cake with hazelnut craquelin (brittle). Shape small chestnuts out of chestnut paste and dip them in tempered couverture chocolate. Make leaves out of marzipan or pulled sugar. Place these decorations at the center of the cake.

# Spanish Orange

## Recipes

### Chocolate/Orange Sponge Cake

600 g almond paste (21 oz.)
140 g (7) egg yolks (5 oz.)
250 g (5) eggs (9 oz.)
zests of three oranges
550 g egg whites (19.5 oz.)
200 g confectioners' sugar (7 oz.)
50 g cocoa powder (1.5 oz.)

### Orange Mousse

500 g sugar (17.5 oz.) plus 150 ml water
 (5 fl. oz.), cooked to 120°C (248°F)
10 egg whites, beaten to firm peaks
100 g glucose (3.5 oz.)
500 ml orange juice (17 fl. oz.)
20 ml lemon juice (4 tsp.)
24 g gelatin (3/4 oz.)
1 L heavy cream (34 fl. oz.), whipped

### Orange Cream

600 g pastry cream (21 oz.)
zests of ten oranges
16 g gelatin (1/2 oz.)
800 ml heavy cream (27 fl. oz.), whipped

### Cointreau-flavored Sugar Syrup

350 ml sugar syrup (12 fl. oz.), at
 1260 D
200 ml Cointreau (6.5 fl. oz.)
100 ml orange juice (3.5 fl. oz.)

### Assembling the Cake

Place a metal cake ring that is 3 to 4 cm (1.25 to 1.5 in.) high over a cardboard circle.

Line the inside of the ring with halved candied orange slices. Place a thin layer of orange cream inside the ring, over the cardboard, and spread the cream around the inside of the ring as well.

Place a layer of chocolate/orange sponge cake over the cream and brush it with Cointreau-flavored sugar syrup.

Add a layer of orange cream over the sponge cake so that the ring is half full.

Fill the ring to the rim with orange mousse and place the cake in the freezer.

Once the cake is frozen, remove the cake ring by warming it.

### Decoration

Glaze the top of the cake with orange glaze. Place a fluted, candied orange slice in the center.

## Presentation

The Spanish orange is a cool, light cake appropriate to serve at the end of a fine meal. This cake can be made throughout the year. The entire cake is flavored with orange, making it particularly appealing to those who enjoy this flavor.

## Composition

Fresh oranges
Chocolate/orange sponge cake
Orange mousse
Orange cream
Cointreau-flavored sugar syrup
Orange glaze
Candied orange slices

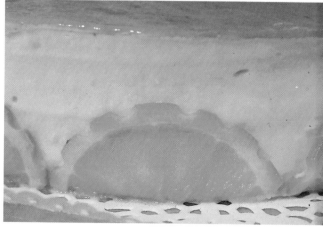

# Le rêve de Montmorency

## Presentation

The rêve de Montmorency (dream of Montmorency) is appropriately named. Montmorency is a region in France where cherries are popular. This is a colorful cake best made when fresh cherries are available. This cake combines a smooth cherry bavarian with a layer of rich cherry-flavored ganache.

## Composition

Cherry sponge cake
Cherry ganache
Kirsch bavarian
Fresh and candied cherries
Chantilly cream
Cherry-flavored sugar syrup

## Recipes

### Cherry Sponge Cake

250 g almond paste (9 oz.)
50 g candied cherries (1.5 oz.)
6 egg yolks - 2 eggs
100 g cornstarch (3.5 oz.)
100 g cake flour (3.5 oz.)

6 egg whites, beaten to firm peaks
125 g sugar (4.5 oz.)

### Cherry Ganache

700 g dark chocolate (24.5 oz.)
500 ml heavy cream (17 fl. oz.)
100 ml Kirsch (3.5 fl. oz.)

### Kirsch Bavarian

600 ml milk (21 fl. oz.)
8 egg yolks
150 g sugar (5 oz.)
16 g gelatin (1/2 oz.)
500 ml heavy cream (17 fl. oz.), whipped
50 ml Kirsch (1.5 fl. oz.)

### Cherry-flavored Sugar Syrup

300 ml sugar syrup (10 fl. oz.), at 1260 D
200 ml Kirsch (6.5 fl. oz.)

### Assembling the Cake

Place a cake ring that is 3 to 4 cm (1.25 to 1.5 in.) high over a cardboard circle.

Line the ring with cherry sponge cake. Place a layer of cherry sponge cake over the bottom of the cardboard, and brush all the sponge cake with cherry-flavored sugar syrup. Place a layer of cherry ganache over the sponge cake, and cover with a second layer of sponge cake. Brush with cherry-flavored sugar syrup.

Place a layer of Kirsch bavarian in the ring. Push fresh or candied cherries into the bavarian at the edge of the cake. Place a third layer of cherry sponge cake over the cream, and brush it with cherry-flavored sugar syrup.

Fill the cake almost to the rim of the ring with Kirsch bavarian and again press a ring of cherries into the cream at the edge. Fill the cake to the rim (so the cherries are covered) with the Kirsch bavarian. Place the cake in the freezer until set or needed.

### Decoration

Remove the metal cake ring and decorate the top of the cake with circles of fresh cherries alternated with rings of Chantilly cream, using a pastry bag with a fluted tip.

# Modern desserts by François Bastien

## François Bastien

*François Bastien is the owner and pastry chef of the highly respected pastry shop Maison Edeline-Bastien, located in Paris.*

*Mr. Bastien has been honored with the title Compagnon du Tour de France, which indicates he has trained and worked with some of the finest pastry chefs throughout France.*

*The four desserts presented by Mr. Bastien in this section show how he creatively adapts traditional techniques without being swayed by the latest trends in the field.*

# Le nougat de Tours

### Recipes

For 4 cakes serving 6 to 7 each, or 15 individual cakes

### Almond Meringue

25 egg whites, beaten to firm peaks
100 g sugar (3.5 oz.), to stiffen the beaten egg whites
  Carefully fold 500 g almond powder (17.5 oz.), 400 g sugar (14 oz.), and the raisins previously macerated in rum into the meringue.

### Preparation

  Line the tart ring with sweetened tart dough.

### Assembling the Cake

  Fill the tart ring (lined with sweetened tart dough) to the rim with the almond meringue.
  Sprinkle the meringue with confectioners' sugar twice, allowing the first layer to penetrate the cake before sprinkling on the second layer.

### Baking

  Bake the cake in a moderate oven at 180°C (350°F).
  After baking, remove the tart ring and place the cake on a cardboard circle.

### Presentation

  The nougat de Tours (Tours is a French town) is based on a light almond meringue. This cake is easy to transport and stores well.

### Composition

Pâte sucrée (sweetened tart dough)
Apricot preserves
Raisins macerated in rum
Almond meringue
Confectioners' sugar

# Le Trocadéro

## Presentation

The Trocadéro is a rich dessert combining layers of coffee macaroon and a smooth, light-textured chocolate ganache.

Without decoration, this cake freezes well, making it possible to prepare several cakes at a time in advance.

## Composition

Coffee macaroon
Light ganache
Couverture chocolate
Dark-chocolate shavings
Confectioners' sugar

## Recipes

For 4 cakes serving 6 to 7 each

### Coffee Macaroon

12 egg whites
500 g almond powder (17.5 oz.)
500 g confectioners' sugar (17.5 oz.)
100 g instant coffee granules (3.5 oz.)

### Light Ganache

1 kg couverture chocolate (35 oz.)
1 kg milk chocolate (35 oz.)
30 g instant coffee granules (1 oz.)
1 L heavy cream (34 fl. oz.), whipped

## Preparation

Prepare the coffee macaroon batter. Pipe it out to the desired size on a sheet pan covered with parchment paper, using a pastry bag and small plain tip.

After the macaroon circles are baked, pour a small amount of water between the sheet pan and parchment paper on which the macaroon circles were baked. This will make removing the macaroon circles very easy. Be careful not to get the macaroon wet.

## Assembling the Cake

Place a metal cake ring that is 4 to 5 cm (1.5 to 2 in.) high over a cardboard circle.

Place a layer of coffee macaroon, cut 2 cm (3/4 in.) smaller than the metal cake ring, into the ring.

Fill the ring one-third full with the light ganache and place a second layer of macaroon, slightly smaller in diameter than the first, over it.

Fill the ring with a second layer of light ganache, so it is two-thirds full.

Place a third layer of coffee macaroon, the same diameter as the second, over the ganache.

Fill the ring to the rim with the light ganache and level the surface with a metal spatula.

Place the cake in the freezer to set.

When the cake is to be decorated, remove the metal cake ring by warming the outside with a hot towel or small propane torch.

## Decoration

Place a band of tempered couverture chocolate around the cake.

Place large shavings made from tempered couverture chocolate on top of the cake.

Lightly dust the top of the cake with confectioners' sugar.

# Le Montmartre

## Presentation

The Montmartre (named for a section of Paris) is a real chocolate lover's dessert, as it is made entirely out of white and dark chocolate. This cake freezes well without decoration, which should be added as needed before serving.

## Composition

Chocolate meringue
Chocolate mousse
White-chocolate shavings
White-chocolate band
Confectioners' sugar

## Recipes

For 4 cakes, serving 6 to 7 each

### Chocolate Meringue

12 egg whites
1200 g granulated sugar (42.5 oz.)
100 g cocoa powder (3.5 oz.)

### Chocolate Mousse

500 ml vanilla bombe batter (17 fl. oz.)
1 kg chocolate (35 oz.), melted, plus
    500 ml warm water (17 fl. oz.) added
    to the chocolate and cooled
1.5 L heavy cream (50.5 fl. oz.), whipped

### Preparation

Make two chocolate meringue circles per cake, 2 cm (3/4 in.) smaller than the metal cake ring.

### Assembling the Cake

Place a metal cake ring that is 4 to 5 cm (1.5 to 2 in.) high over a cardboard circle.

Place a layer of chocolate meringue inside the ring, over the cardboard.

Fill the ring with a layer of chocolate mousse and place a second layer of chocolate meringue over the mousse.

Fill the ring to the rim with the chocolate mousse, and smooth the surface with a metal spatula.

Place the cake in the freezer until set.

When the cake is needed, remove the ring by warming the outside. Make sure the cake is firmly set or frozen before removing the ring.

## Decoration

Place a band made from tempered white chocolate around the side of the cake.

Place shavings made from tempered white chocolate on top of the cake, and lightly sprinkle the top with confectioners' sugar.

When appropriate, place a piece of chocolate imprinted with the name of the pastry shop in the center of the cake.

# Le Brésilien

### Coffee Meringue

1 kg sugar (35 oz.) plus 300 ml water (10 fl. oz.), cooked to 120°C (248°F)
500 ml (16) egg whites (17 fl. oz.)
500 g confectioners' sugar (17.5 oz.)
coffee extract

### Coffee Mousse

1 L milk (34 fl. oz.)
250 g sugar (9 oz.)
14 egg yolks
24 sheets (48 g) gelatin (1.5 oz.)
1.5 L heavy cream (50.5 fl. oz.), whipped
coffee extract

### Preparation

Make the coffee macaroons and the sticks of coffee meringue.

Make one circle of chocolate meringue per cake, piped out with a pastry bag fitted with no. 7 plain tip.

### Assembling the Cake

Place a metal cake ring that is 4 to 5 cm (1.5 to 2 in.) high over a cardboard circle.

Place a layer of chocolate meringue, 2 cm (3/4 in.) smaller in diameter than the cake ring, over the cardboard inside the ring.

Fill the ring halfway with coffee mousse, and set the sticks of coffee meringue horizontally in the mousse.

Fill the ring to the rim with the coffee mousse and smooth the surface with a metal spatula.

Place the cake in the freezer to set.

After the cake is firmly set or frozen, remove the cake ring by warming it with a small propane torch.

### Decoration

Cover the entire cake with coffee macaroons just before it is presented.

### Presentation

The Brésilien is a cake that can be served throughout the year. This cake is flavored almost entirely with coffee, except for a base of chocolate meringue. There is no liquor in this cake.

Without its decoration of coffee macaroons, this cake freezes very well.

### Composition

Chocolate meringue
Coffee mousse
Coffee meringue sticks
Coffee macaroons

### Recipes

For 4 cakes, serving 6 to 7 each

### Chocolate Meringue

10 egg whites, beaten to firm peaks
1 kg sugar (35 oz.) plus 300 ml water (10 fl. oz.), cooked to 120°C (248°F)

After the meringue is cooled, add:
40 g confectioners' sugar (1.5 oz.)
360 g cocoa powder (12.5 oz.), dissolved in a small amount of sugar syrup at 1260 D to make it easier to incorporate

### Coffee Macaroons

1 kg confectioners' sugar (35 oz.)
500 g almond powder (17.5 oz.)
15 g instant coffee granules (1/2 oz.)
500 ml egg whites (17 fl. oz.)

# Modern desserts by Denis Ruffel

## Denis Ruffel

Denis Ruffel is a young yet well-known and respected experienced professional in the field of pastry making. He has won several awards in competitions, including the Culinary Trophy and Meilleur Chef de l'année (best chef of the year).

Mr. Ruffel has been working professionally for over ten years and helped develop the well-known pastry shop Maison Millet in Paris, France.

Denis Ruffel is the author of the series L'Artisan Traiteur, about catering.

# Vallée d'Auge

## Presentation

The vallée d'auge is a somewhat seasonal dessert, usually served during the fall and winter months when apples are in season.

As this cake freezes well, it is possible to prepare several at a time, decorating and serving them as needed.

## Composition

Strips of sponge cake
Almond sponge cake (joconde biscuit)
Calvados-flavored sugar syrup
Apple mousse
Apple slices, baked and flambéed
Apple jelly flavored with Calvados
Prune puree

## Recipes

For 25 to 30 servings

### Joconde Biscuit (Almond Sponge Cake)

For three sheets of sponge cake
    40 × 60 cm (16 × 24 in.)

780 g tant pour tant (27.5 oz)—equal amounts of almond powder and sugar
8 eggs
80 g flour (3 oz.)
9 egg whites, beaten to firm peaks
75 g butter (2.5 oz.), melted

### Apple Mousse

1 L apple cider (34 fl. oz.), reduced to 100 ml (3.5 fl. oz.)
10 sheets (20 g) gelatin (1/2 oz.)
700 g apple puree (24.5 oz.), lightly sweetened and reduced
150 ml Calvados (5 fl. oz.)
750 ml heavy cream (26.5 fl. oz.), whipped
Italian meringue: 5 egg whites, beaten to firm peaks, plus 200 g sugar (7 oz.) and 50 ml water (1.5 fl. oz.), cooked to 122°C (251°F)

### Calvados-flavored Sugar Syrup

500 ml sugar syrup (17 fl. oz.), at 1260 D
100 ml Calvados (3.5 fl. oz.)

## Preparation

Cut strips of sponge cake to the height of the mold. Brush them with prune puree and stack them so they stick together. Brush with Calvados-flavored sugar syrup.

Bake the joconde (almond) biscuit in a tart ring that is the same diameter as the cake ring to be used for assembling the cake.

Prepare the apples: peel, rub with lemon, and slice.

Butter and sprinkle a Teflon or other nonstick sheet pan (or sauté pan) with white and brown sugar. Place the apple slices over the sugar and butter and place more butter and white and brown sugar over them.

Place the apples in a hot oven and bake until tender. Flambé them with Calvados after removing them from the oven.

Allow the apple slices to cool before using them.

## Assembling the Cake

Line a génoise cake mold to the rim with 5-mm-thick (1/4-in.) strips of the sponge cake/prune puree "sandwiches" that have been soaked in Calvados-flavored sugar syrup.

Form a rosette with the baked, flambéed apple slices on the bottom of the génoise mold.

Cover the apple slices with apple mousse, one-third of the way up the mold. Place baked apple slices over the mousse and cover the slices with more mousse, almost to the rim of the mold.

Place a layer of joconde (almond) biscuit over the mousse and brush it lightly with Calvados-flavored sugar syrup.

Place the cake in the freezer until set.

Unmold the cake when needed by turning it onto a cardboard circle. The top becomes the bottom, as the cake was constructed upside down.

## Decoration

Glaze the top of the cake with an apple jelly flavored with Calvados.

# Méli-Mélo

## Presentation

The Méli-Mélo cake is assembled with a layer of fruit in the middle of the cake. Serve this cake along with a passion-fruit coulis laced with vodka and with a sprinkling of passion-fruit seeds.

This cake is especially suitable during the warmer months, as it is refreshing and the tropical fruits that garnish the cake are more readily available. The Méli-Mélo freezes well and should be decorated with fresh fruit when served.

## Composition

Chocolate-covered almond succès meringue
Almond sponge cake
Tropical bavarian
Rum-flavored sugar syrup
Garniture of fresh fruit, including pineapple, mango, and kiwi
Decoration of fresh fruit including pineapple, mango, kiwi, banana, orange, and strawberry

## Recipes

### Succès Meringue

10 egg whites
500 g granulated sugar (17.5 oz.)
150 g almond powder (5 oz.) plus 150 g sugar (5 oz.) plus 25 g powdered milk (1 oz.) with 25 percent fat, all sifted together

### Almond Sponge Cake

300 g almond paste (10.5 oz.)
100 g confectioners' sugar (3.5 oz.)
8 egg yolks, 8 egg whites, 2 eggs
180 g cornstarch (6.5 oz.)
75 g butter (2.5 oz.), melted

### Tropical Bavarian

1 L milk (34 fl. oz.)
200 g sugar (7 oz.)
two vanilla beans
24 egg yolks

18 sheets (36 g) gelatin (1 oz.)
200 ml rum (6.5 fl. oz.)
1.5 L heavy cream (50.5 fl. oz.)

### Rum-flavored Sugar Syrup

500 ml sugar syrup (17 fl. oz.), at 1260 D
150 ml rum (5 fl. oz.)

## Preparation

Make the almond sponge cake.
Make the succès. After cooling, coat it with tempered couverture chocolate.
Prepare the fruit to be placed inside the cake: poach thin slices of pineapple in a light syrup, cut slices of mango and kiwi. Other fruits can also be used.

## Assembling the Cake

Place a metal cake ring that is 6 cm (2.5 in.) high over a cardboard circle of the same diameter.
Place a layer of chocolate-covered succès, 2 cm (3/4 in.) smaller in diameter than the ring, over the cardboard, inside the ring.
Fill the ring one-third full with tropical bavarian.
Carefully arrange the assorted fruits over the bavarian. Cover the fruit with a second layer of tropical bavarian so the ring is now two-thirds full.
Place a layer of almond sponge cake over the bavarian, and brush it with rum-flavored sugar syrup.
Fill the ring to the rim with the tropical bavarian and smooth the surface with a metal spatula.
Place the cake in the freezer until set or frozen. When the cake is to be used, remove the ring by heating it on the outside with a small propane torch.

## Decoration

Press grated toasted coconut around the side of the cake.
Decorate the top of the cake with assorted fruit, arranging the fruit in a colorful and attractive way.
With a pastry brush, glaze the fruit with passion-fruit jelly.

# Mille-feuilles de fruits rouges

## Presentation

Mille-feuilles translates literally as a thousand layers, signifying the layers of puff pastry that make up what are known as napoleons in English. The assorted red fruit in this cake make it very delicate and colorful.

Once assembled, this cake does not hold up well, and so it should be prepared just before serving.

Serve the cake with a red-fruit coulis.

## Composition

Two thin circles of puff pastry (mille-feuilles)
Strawberries, raspberries, and wild strawberries
Honey mousseline
Small circles of puff pastry
Mint leaves

## Recipe

### Honey Mousseline
*Pastry Cream*

500 ml milk (17 fl. oz.)
1 vanilla bean
100 g sugar (3.5 oz.)
12 egg yolks
30 g flour (1 oz.)
30 g cornstarch (1 oz.)
75 g butter (2.5 oz.)

*Gelatin*

15 sheets (30 g) gelatin (1 oz.), dissolved in 90 ml water (3 oz) plus 90 g sugar (3 oz.)

*Honey Italian Meringue*

2 egg whites
120 g honey (4 oz.), cooked to 120°C (248°F)

*Whipped Cream*

500 ml heavy cream (17 fl. oz.), whipped

## Preparation

Prepare two rounds of puff pastry. Bake them in a hot oven at 250°C (500°F). Toward the end of baking, glaze them by generously sprinkling with confectioners' sugar.

Cut small rounds of puff pastry for decoration from a sheet of puff pastry dough with a fluted cutter, and bake.

## Assembling the Cake

Place a 5-cm-high (2-in.) metal cake ring over a cardboard circle.

Line the inside of the ring with a strip of clear plastic cut to the same size as the ring.

Place one of the puff pastry circles inside the ring, over the cardboard.

Line the inside of the ring with strawberries cut in half lengthwise so the cut half is lying flat against the plastic strip.

Fill the ring half full with the honey mousseline, using a pastry bag fitted with a no. 7 tip.

Cover the mousseline with a layer of raspberries and wild strawberries.

Fill the cake almost to the rim with honey mousseline.

Cover the cake with the second circle of puff pastry, with the glazed side facing up.

## Decoration

Decorate the small puff pastry rounds by piping out honey mousseline on top using a pastry bag and setting cut mint leaves and cut strawberries or other red fruit into the mousseline.

Place the decorated rounds of puff pastry in a circle on top of the cake.

Remove the metal cake ring and plastic before serving.

# Charlotte au chocolat

### Presentation

A charlotte is usually a cake supported with sponge cake or ladyfingers around the side, filled with a light filling. This charlotte is filled with chocolate bavarian.

Serve this charlotte with crème anglaise presented on the side in a sauce boat.

This cake freezes well and should be decorated with chocolate shavings just before servng.

### Composition

Sponge cake rounds
Strips of chocolate/vanilla sponge cake
Chocolate bavarian
Vanilla-flavored sugar syrup
White-chocolate curls
Dark-chocolate shavings
Confectioners' sugar
Cocoa powder

### Recipes

#### Sponge Cake

8 egg whites
250 g sugar (9 oz.)
8 egg yolks
250 g cake flour (9 oz.)

#### Vanilla-flavored Sugar Syrup

500 ml sugar syrup (17 fl. oz.), at 1260 D
20 ml vanilla extract (1.5 Tbsp.)

### Chocolate Bavarian

1 L milk (34 fl. oz.)
One vanilla bean
130 g bittersweet couverture chocolate (4.5 oz.)
130 g cocoa powder (4.5 oz.)
16 egg yolks
300 g sugar (10.5 oz.)
16 sheets (32 g) gelatin (1 oz.)
1 L heavy cream (34 fl. oz.)
Italian meringue: 8 egg whites plus 375 g sugar (13 oz.) plus 100 ml water (3.5 oz.), cooked to 122°C (251°F), plus 50 g cocoa powder (1.5 oz.)

### Preparation

Using two pastry bags with no. 7 tips, one filled with chocolate sponge cake batter, the other with vanilla sponge cake batter, and pipe out alternating diagonal strips of vanilla and chocolate batter onto a sheet pan covered with parchment paper.

Make the sponge cake rounds.

### Assembling the Cake

Place a metal cake ring that is 6 cm (2.5 in.) high over a cardboard circle.

Line the ring to the rim with a strip of vanilla/chocolate sponge cake.

Place a round of sponge cake inside the ring over the cardboard. Brush the sponge cake base and sides with vanilla-flavored sugar syrup.

Using a ladle, fill the ring to the rim with chocolate bavarian.

Place the cake in the freezer until set or needed.

Remove the metal cake ring before decorating.

### Decoration

The charlotte is decorated with white and dark chocolate on top to complement the theme of vanilla and chocolate sponge cake around the cake.

Place white-chocolate curls around the edge of the top of the cake. Place dark-chocolate shavings in the center, inside the border of white-chocolate curls.

Lightly dust the white-chocolate curls with cocoa powder and dust the dark-chocolate shavings with confectioners' sugar.

# Modern desserts by Henri Raimbault

## Henri Raimbault

*Henri Raimbault is known throughout France and internationally. He has won some of the most difficult competitions in his field, most notably the Meilleur Ouvrier de France.*

*Henri Raimbault works as the pastry chef for Patisfrance, one of the largest international pastry-supply companies.*

# La Chocolette

### Presentation

The chocolette is a rich classical dessert that is usually served during the colder months. This cake is assembled in sheets, making it possible to change the size and shape of the cake easily as needed.

### Almond Rocher (Meringue) Bases

8 egg whites - 150 g confectioners' sugar (5 oz.), to stiffen the meringue
350 g sugar (12.5 oz.) plus 100 ml water (3.5 fl. oz.), cooked to 120°C (248°F)
250 g sliced almonds (9 oz.)

### Sponge Cake

10 egg whites, 250 g sugar (9 oz.)
10 egg yolks, 250 g cake flour (9 oz.)

### Chocolate Sponge Cake

10 egg whites, 300 g sugar (10.5 oz.)
Ten egg yolks
225 g cake flour (8 oz.) plus 25 g cocoa powder (1 oz.), sifted together

### Rum Ganache

1 L crème fraîche or heavy cream (34 fl. oz.)
1200 g chocolate (42.5 oz.)
200 ml rum (6.5 fl. oz.)

### Ganache Glaze

1 L crème fraîche or heavy cream (34 fl. oz.)
1 kg couverture chocolate (35 oz.)

### Rum-flavored Sugar Syrup

1 L sugar syrup (34 fl. oz.), at 1260 D
100 ml rum (3.5 fl. oz.)

### Assembling the Cake

Place a piece of parchment paper on a sheet pan; a square cake frame can be placed over the parchment paper if available.

Place a layer of almond rocher on the sheet pan inside the frame (if used) and spread on a layer of rum ganache approximately 5 mm (1/4 in.) thick. Place a layer of chocolate sponge cake over the ganache, upside down so it can better absorb the syrup. Brush the sponge cake with rum-flavored sugar syrup.

Over the sponge cake, spread a second layer of rum ganache about 5 mm (1/4 in.) thick. Place a layer of plain sponge cake over the ganache and brush it with rum-flavored sugar syrup.

Allow the syrup to penetrate the sponge cake before cutting. From the large assembled piece, cut as many cakes needed to the desired sizes. Place the cut cakes over cardboard cut to the same size. Spread a thin layer of rum ganache over the cakes using a metal spatula, and place them in the refrigerator or freezer to set.

# Le Saint-Ghalais

## Presentation

The Saint-Ghalais is a very velvety, soft, and delicate cake.

This cake can be made throughout the year, and it stores well.

## Composition

Soft coconut meringue
Praliné butter cream
Génoise sheet
Rum-flavored sugar syrup
Roasted sliced almonds
Couverture chocolate

## Recipes

### Soft Coconut Meringue

16 egg whites, beaten to firm peaks, plus
350 g sugar (12.5 oz.), added in small amounts to the egg whites as they are being beaten, with most added when the peaks are firm.
250 g grated coconut (9 oz.)

Spread a 1.5-cm (1/2-in.) layer of the coconut meringue over a buttered, floured nonstick sheet pan. A square metal frame can be placed over the sheet pan and moistened with water. Lightly sprinkle the meringue with confectioners' sugar.

Bake the meringue in a moderate oven at 200°C (375°F) for 5 minutes with the door closed, then for 15 minutes with the oven door open to allow the moisture to escape.

### Praliné Butter Cream

200 g praline paste (7 oz.)
500 g butter cream (17.5 oz.)

### Génoise Sheet

8 eggs
250 g sugar (9 oz.)
250 g cake flour (9 oz.)

### Rum-flavored Sugar Syrup

300 ml sugar syrup (10 fl. oz.), at 1260 D
100 ml water (3.5 fl. oz.)
100 ml rum (3.5 fl. oz.)

### Assembling the Cake

Wait until the coconut meringue is completely cool before assembling the cake.

Spread a layer of praliné butter cream approximately 5 mm (1/4 in.) thick over the coconut meringue.

Over the butter cream, place a layer of génoise, upside down, so that it will more easily absorb the syrup. Brush it with rum-flavored sugar syrup.

Spread on a second layer of praliné butter cream.

Place a second layer of coconut meringue over the butter cream, with the golden side up.

Place the cake in the refrigerator or freezer to set.

Cut the large cake to make smaller cakes to the sizes desired, in squares or rectangles.

## Decoration

Spread the sides of each cake with praliné butter cream and press roasted, sliced almonds around the sides.

Fill a paper cone with couverture chocolate and draw lines quickly across the top of the cake.

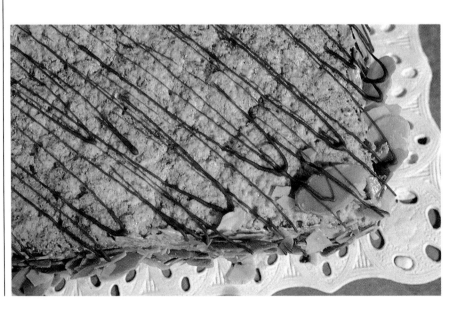

# Modern desserts by Jean Creveux

# Miroirs des quatre saisons (Mirrors of the four seasons)

### Presentation

The miroirs des quatre saisons all share the same base made from succès/progrès (almond/hazelnut meringue) and almond cream. Each dessert is filled and decorated differently to represent a different season. As this is a particularly difficult preparation, greater detail is given to the preparation and decoration of these desserts on pages 222 to 223.

These four cakes are particularly appreciated by those who prefer classic desserts rather than exotic, newer cakes.

It is possible to make all four of the cakes and present them in a pastry shop window or to serve them for a special occasion or reception, as they are strikingly beautiful and complement each other well.

## Jean Creveux

*Jean Creveux is a true master of French pastry. He has received all the highest honorary titles possible in his field, including Meilleur Ouvrier de France after winning the most difficult and distinguished competition for pastry chefs in France.*

*Jean Creveux is a director of CFA of Vincennes, which is a pastry school in Paris, and continues to apply his experience and talent to help promote the field of pastry making.*

# Miroir de Printemps (Mirror of Spring)

**Composition**

Succès-progrès (see page 222)
Strawberry-flavored sugar syrup

Strawberry bavarian
Strawberry glaze
Chantilly cream

### Strawberry Bavarian

1 L strawberry pulp or strained strawberry pulp (34 fl. oz.)
1 L sugar syrup (34 fl. oz.), at 1260 D
juice of one lemon
16 sheets (32 g) gelatin (1 oz.)
1.5 L heavy cream (50.5 fl. oz.), whipped

### Strawberry-flavored Sugar Syrup

500 g strawberry pulp (17 fl. oz.)
400 ml sugar syrup (13.5 fl. oz.), at
1260 D
100 ml strawberry liqueur (3.5 fl. oz.)

### Strawberry Glaze

1 L strawberry pulp (34 fl. oz.)
500 g sugar (17.5 oz.)
8 sheets (16 g) gelatin (1/2 oz.)

### Chantilly Cream

1 L heavy cream (34 fl. oz.)
150 g confectioners' sugar (5 oz.)
10 g vanilla sugar (2 tsp.)

### Assembling the Cake

(See page 222 for greater detail.)

Place a metal cake ring that is 3 to 4
cm (1 to 1.5 in.) high over a cardboard
circle and place a layer of succès/progrès
inside the ring. Brush the center of the
succès/progrès with strawberry-flavored
sugar syrup.

Cut strawberries in half. Line the peri-
meter of the ring with the halved strawberries; stand them on the stem ends,
with the cut sides facing out, flat against
the wall of the cake ring.

Fill the ring to the rim with strawberry
bavarian. Sprinkle pieces of succès/pro-
grès soaked in strawberry-flavored sugar
syrup over the bavarian, pressing some
pieces into the bavarian.

Chill the cake to set it. Remove the
cake ring.

To decorate, using a pastry bag, pipe
out Chantilly cream around the sides,
between the strawberries. Place the top
layer of succès/progrès atop the cake.
Decorate the center with strawberry slices, brush them with strawberry glaze,
and pipe a ring of Chantilly cream
around them.

# Miroir d'Eté (Mirror of Summer)

### Assorted-Fruit Bavarian

1 L sugar syrup (34 fl. oz.), at 1260 D
1 L fruit pulp made from equal parts crushed and strained pears, peaches, and apricots (34 fl. oz.)
juice of one lemon
16 sheets (32 g) gelatin (1 oz.)
1.5 L heavy cream (50.5 fl. oz.)

### Fruit-flavored Sugar Syrup

Apricot and pear juice, sweetened to make a syrup at 1260 D and flavored with apricot liqueur or pear liquor

### Jelly Glaze

1 kg apricot glaze (35 oz.)
50 g glucose (1.5 oz.)
100 ml pear liqueur (3.5 fl. oz.)
juice of one lemon

### Chantilly Cream

1 L heavy cream (34 fl. oz.)
150 g confectioners' sugar (5 oz.)
10 g vanilla sugar (2 tsp.)

### Assembling the Cake

(See page 222 for greater detail.)

Place a metal cake ring that is 3 to 4 cm (1 to 1.5 in.) high over a cardboard circle. Place the bottom layer of succès/progrès inside the cake ring. Brush the succès/progrès with apricot/pear syrup.

Place assorted cut fruits atop the succès/progrès.

Fill the ring to the rim with the fruit bavarian. Sprinkle pieces of fruit and succès/progrès soaked in fruit-flavored sugar syrup over the bavarian.

Chill the cake to set it.

Remove the metal cake ring when the cake is set. To decorate, pipe Chantilly cream around its sides, and press poached pears and peaches, candied cherries, and angelica into the cream.

Place the top layer of succès/progrès on the cake and put assorted fruit in the center. Brush the fruit with the jelly glaze. Pipe a ring of Chantilly cream around the fruit. A pulled-sugar flower may be placed on top of the cake.

**Composition**

Succès/progrès (see page 222)
Fruit-flavored sugar syrup

Assorted-fruit bavarian
Jelly glaze
Chantilly cream

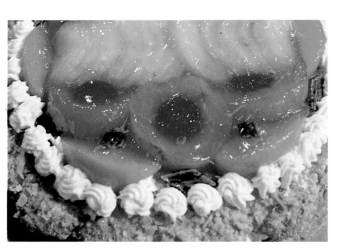

# Miroir d'Automne (Mirror of Autumn)

### Composition

Succès/progrès (see page 222 to 223)
Coffee-flavored sugar syrup

Coffter cream
Apricot glaze
Liqueur-filled coffee bean candies
Royal icing

### Coffee Butter Cream

1 kg butter (35 oz.)
800 g sugar (28 oz.) plus 200 ml water
(6.5 fl. oz.), cooked to 120°C (248°F)
5 egg yolks
4 eggs
30 ml coffee extract (1 fl. oz.)

### Coffee-flavored Sugar Syrup

1 L sugar syrup (34 fl. oz.), at 1260 D
80 g coffee beans (3 oz.), infused in the
sugar syrup as it comes to a boil, *or*
coffee extract to taste

### Apricot Glaze

1 kg apricot nappage (35 oz.)
50 g glucose (1.5 oz.)

### Royal Icing

1 egg white
150 g confectioners' sugar (5 oz.)

### Assembling the Cake

(See page 223 for greater detail.)
Brush the bottom layer of succès/progrès with coffee-flavored sugar syrup.

Using a pastry bag and medium fluted tip, pipe rosettes of coffee butter cream around the edge of the succès/progrès. Pipe out more coffee butter cream, to cover the entire layer.

Place several liqueur-filled coffee bean candies and pieces of succès/progrès soaked in coffee-flavored sugar syrup on top of and into the butter cream.

Place the top layer of succès/progrès over the butter cream.

To decorate, glaze the top of the cake with a large circle of apricot glaze to create a mirror effect. Small circles of glaze can be placed around the edge of the top of the cake. Using a paper cone, pipe royal icing around the circles of apricot glaze; leaves can also be painted onto the circles with food coloring. A pulled-sugar flower and leaves can be placed in the center of the cake.

The apricot glaze can be replaced with water or rum glaze.

# Miroir d'Hiver (Mirror of Winter)

### Hazelnut Ganache

1 kg chocolate (35 oz.)
1 L crème fraîche or heavy cream (34 fl. oz.), whipped
125 g praline paste (4.5 oz.)
several drops of coffee extract
100 g nougatine pieces (3.5 oz.)

### Rum or Grand Marnier–flavored Sugar Syrup

1 L sugar syrup (34 fl. oz.), at 1260 D
300 ml rum or Grand Marnier (10 fl. oz.)

### Apricot Glaze

1 kg apricot nappage (35 oz.)
50 g glucose (1.5 oz.)

### Royal Icing

1 egg white
150 g confectioners' sugar (3.5 oz.)

### Assembling the Cake

(See page 223 for greater detail.)

Brush the center of the succès/progrès with rum or Grand Marnier–flavored sugar syrup.

Using a pastry bag with a medium fluted tip (the teeth of the tip should be closely spaced), pipe out rosettes of hazelnut ganache around the border; then cover the whole base with ganache.

Sprinkle the top of the ganache with nougatine pieces and pieces of succès/progrès soaked in sugar syrup.

Place the top layer of succès/progrès over the cake.

To decorate, make a large circle of apricot glaze in center of the cake and smaller circles around the edge.

Using a paper cone, pipe royal icing around the circles of glaze. Paint leaves inside the circles of glaze with food coloring and a paint brush. Place pulled-sugar leaves and ribbons on top of the cake.

The apricot glaze can be replaced with water or rum glaze.

## Composition

| | |
|---|---|
| Succès/progrès (see pages 222 to 223) | Hazelnut ganache |
| Rum or Grand Marnier–flavored sugar syrup | Nougatine pieces |
| | Apricot glaze |
| | Royal icing |

# Assembling and decorating

### Making the Succès/Progrès Layers

It is imperative that the egg whites are beaten to firm peaks when making the succès/progrès so they will hold their shape. The layers cannot be trimmed or shaped after they are baked. It is possible, however, to use the less attractive layer on the bottom of the cake.

Trace two circles on parchment paper or draw an outline on buttered, floured sheet pans to make it easier to pipe out the meringue evenly and to form the fluted edge on which the small mirrors are placed. Use a pastry bag with a plain no 8 tip to pipe out the meringue.

Sprinkle the meringue with chopped almonds, then pipe out a thin layer of almond cream in the center. It is important to use almond cream that is well whipped and to apply only a thin layer so it will not become runny and lose its shape during baking.

Bake the pieces in a dry 200°C (375°F) oven.

**Mirrors of
Spring and Summer**

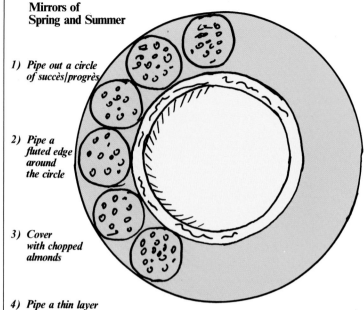

1) *Pipe out a circle of succès/progrès*

2) *Pipe a fluted edge around the circle*

3) *Cover with chopped almonds*

4) *Pipe a thin layer of almond cream in the center*

**Mirrors of Spring and Summer**

**Fresh strawberries**

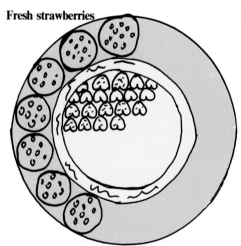

**Sugar flowers**

*Succès/progrès*

*Almond cream*

*Strawberry-flavored sugar syrup*

*Strawberry glaze*

**Sugar flowers**

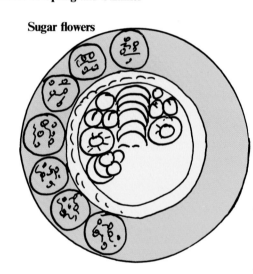

*Succès/progrès*

*Almond cream*

*Fruit-flavored sugar syrup*

*Assorted fruits*

*Glaze*

### Recipe for Succès/Progrès

100 g sugar (3.5 oz.), to stiffen the meringue

16 egg whites

500 g almond powder (17.5 oz.) plus 400 g sugar (14 oz.) plus 50 g cake flour (1.5 oz.)

Beat the egg whites to firm, smooth peaks.

Delicately fold the almond, sugar, and cake flour into the beaten egg whites.

Trace the desired size on parchment paper, or mark buttered, floured sheet pans with the size of the succès/progrès to be baked. Pipe out the batter, carefully, forming an even shape; be especially careful piping out the fluted edge, which can not be trimmed to size after baking. The less attractive of the two layers can serve as the base of the cake.

# the four seasons cakes

## Assembling the Cakes

Brush the center of the succès/progrès, the almond cream, with flavored sugar syrup. The cakes made with fruit (spring and summer) are built in metal cake rings.

Sprinkle the bavarian with a small dice of fruit and pieces of progrès soaked in sugar syrup flavored according to the cake being made.

For the mirror of winter, pipe out rosettes of ganache around the edge of the base using a fluted tip. Fill the center of the base with ganache mixed with pieces of nougatine and pieces of progrès soaked in flavored sugar syrup.

The mirror of autumn is filled with rosettes of coffee butter cream, using a pastry bag and fluted tip. Place several liqueur-filled coffee bean candies and pieces of succès/progrès soaked in flavored sugar syrup in the butter cream in the center of the cake.

It is possible to simplify the decoration of the cake by not making the mirrors and covering the top of the cake with a liqueur- or liquor-flavored glaze such as a rum glaze.

### Mirrors of Autumn and Winter

1) Pipe out a circle of succès/progrès

2) Pipe a fluted edge around the circle

3) Cover with chopped almonds

4) Spread a thin layer of almond cream in the center

*Trace a circle on parchment paper or on a buttered, floured sheet pan*

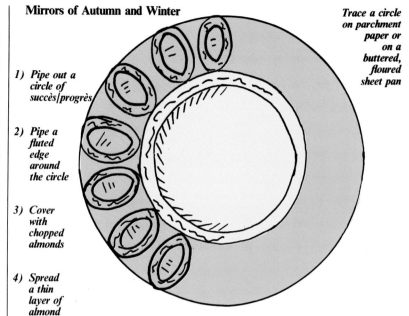

**Mirrors of Autumn and Winter**

### Make small mirrors

Progrès

Almond cream

Flavored sugar syrup

Decorate with flowers or liquor glaze

Progrès

Almond cream

Flavored sugar syrup

Decorate with flowers or liquor glaze

Trace a circle on parchment paper or a buttered, floured sheet pan to serve as a guide for the diameter of the finished succès/progrès. Draw a smaller circle inside the larger one to serve as a guide for the center of the cake; the ring that remains around it (formed by the larger traced circle) will serve as a guide to piping out the fluted edge.

Sprinkle the entire piece with skinless, chopped almonds. Then fill the center of the piece with a thin bayer of almond cream that has been well beaten.

Bake the succès/progrès at 200° C (375° F).

### Recipe for Almond Cream

250 g butter (9 oz.)
250 g sugar (9 oz.)
250 g almond powder (9 oz.)
4 eggs
vanilla sugar

# The importance of pastry decorating

## The Four Seasons: A Prime Example

This volume in the series is dedicated almost entirely to pastry decorating. Jean Creveux's series of cakes representing the four seasons is an excellent example of cake decorating. He has not only made use of possible decoration techniques as explained in this volume but has also used sugar work, as shown in volume 3 of this series. Remember, there are three different levels of decorating.

### Level 1 Decoration: Assembly

This volume presents a variety of pastries and explains how they are assembled. The first level of decoration in pastry making is based on a dessert's composition and assembly—the fillings and doughs used.

### Level 2 Decoration: Classic Techniques

The second level of decoration focuses on the appearance of the dessert based on classic decoration techniques. This level of decoration usually will represent or reinforce the flavors inside the cake. For example, a glaze that is the same flavor as the filling can be used on top of the pastry, or fresh fruits that are the same as the flavor of the filling inside the cake can adorn it.

### Level 3 Decoration: Innovative, Complicated Techniques

This third or highest level of decorating reveals the experience and ability of a professional. It is also at this level that a pastry chef can personalize a dessert, displaying individual taste as well as talent.

The most complex decoration techniques, such as sugar work and chocolate work, are used at this level of decoration, turning a simple dessert into work of art.

**Printemps**

**Été**

**Automne**

**Hiver**

# New Desserts for the 21st century

At the renowned cooking school "Centre Technologique Ferrandi" in Paris, chefs Roland Bilheux and Alain Escoffier preside over the prestigious pastry department. They continue to create new desserts and inspire their young team of teachers to discover new formulas to create exciting combinations of ingredients. Here we present a selection of 12 of the new desserts from this team of experts.

*From left to right :*
**Christian Gillet**
- "Beethoven"
- "Frou-Frou"

**Christophe Majdanski**
- "Cinnamon Tree"
- "Quatre Epices"

**Didier Averty**
- Apple Crumb Tart
- "Pecher Mignon"

**Jean-Roch Therraize**
- "Birmingham"
- Rice Imperial

**Jean-Pierre Lesbats**
- Strawberry Cake
- "Arpajon"

*(not pictured)*
**Thierry Jamard**
- Tropical "Milles Feuilles"
- "Chocolate Hazelnut Cake"

# A guide to

**Rice Impérial**
*(Jean-Roch Therraize)* P. 224

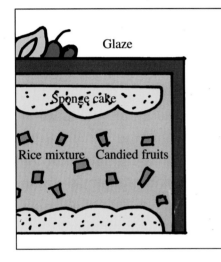

**"Beethoven"**
*(Christian Gillet)* P. 225

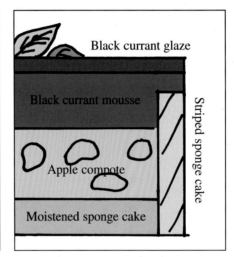

**Birmingham**
*(Jean-Roch Therraize)* P. 226

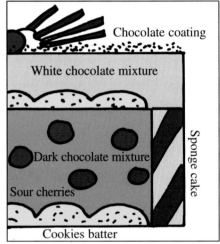

**French Apple Crumbe Tart**
*(Didier Averty)* page 227

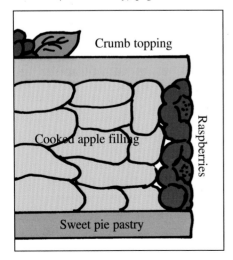

**Hazelnut and Chocolate Mousse**
*(Thierry Jamard)* P. 228

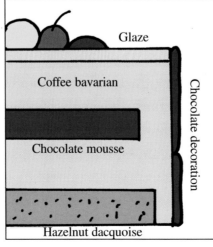

**"Pêcher Mignon"**
*(Didier Averty)* P. 229

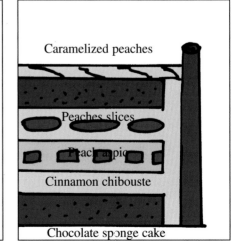

# assembling the desserts

**strawberry cake**
*(Jean-Pierre Lesbats)* P. 230

**Tropical "Mille-feuilles"**
*(Thierry Jamard)* P. 231

**"Cinnamon Tree"**
*(Christophe Majdanski)* P. 232

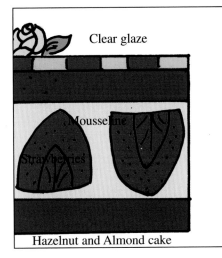

Clear glaze

Mousseline

Strawberries

Hazelnut and Almond cake

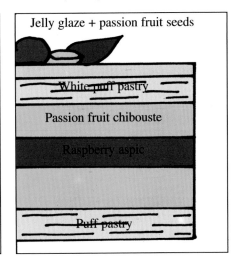

Jelly glaze + passion fruit seeds

White puff pastry

Passion fruit chibouste

Raspberry aspic

Puff pastry

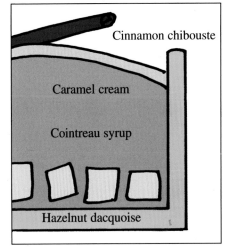

Cinnamon chibouste

Caramel cream

Cointreau syrup

Hazelnut dacquoise

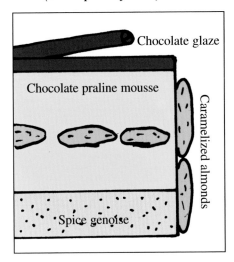

**"Quatre-Epices"**
*(Christophe Majdanski)* P. 233

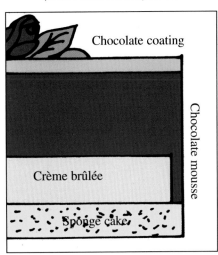

**"Arpajon"**
*(Jean-Pierre Lesbats)* P. 234

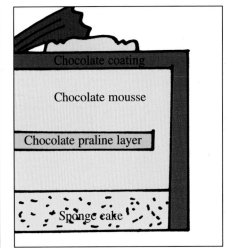

**"Frou-Frou"**
*(Christian Gillet)* P. 235

Chocolate glaze

Chocolate praline mousse

Caramelized almonds

Spice genoise

Chocolate coating

Chocolate mousse

Crème brûlée

Sponge cake

Chocolate coating

Chocolate mousse

Chocolate praline layer

Sponge cake

# Rice Imperial

This is a dessert from the classic French repertoire. The basic recipe can be varied with different fruit and flavorings such as orange, spices (cinnamon, ginger), berries or apples. The sweetness and creaminess of the rice mixture blends very well with tart fruits.

In all preparations of this dish, the secret of the flavor depends on the proper cooking of the rice (which must be round (arborio)).

Rice Imperial should be served very cold and is delicious when enjoyed with a sweet Vouvray or pink Champagne.

## Procedure

Cut the candied fruits into small pieces and cover with Kirsch to macerate.

Prepare the sponge cake batter and pipe out 6 circles measuring 16 cm (5 1/2 in) on parchment paper-lined baking sheets, bake at 190 C (375 F) until golden brown.

Prepare the rice. First blanch the rice by covering with cold water, bringing to a boil then boiling one minute.

Drain and rinse the rice with cold water.

Bring the milk to a boil with the vanilla bean (split). Add the rice, stir then place a teaspoon of butter on top.

Place a circle of parchment paper on top of the rice, put the cover on the pot and cook in a 180 C (350 F) oven until all the liquid is absorbed. Spread the cooked rice onto a hotel pan, cover with plastic wrap and refrigerate. When the rice is cold, stir in the fruits and all the Kirsch.

Make the Bavarian cream and cool until it begins to thicken but is not set.

Combine the chilled rice and cold Bavarian cream (both elements must be cold, otherwise the rice will sink to the bottom).

Fill large or small domed molds with the rice miixture.

Moisten the sponge cakes with flavored syrup and place on top. Cover and refrigerate (do not place in freezer).

## Assembly

Sponge cake base
Molded rice mixture
Raspberry-flavored glaze
Fruit decoration

## Plate presentation

Dip the mold in warm water and unmold onto a platter or plate, glaze the top and decorate with slices of fruits..

Decorate the plate with a medley of red fruits and a little raspberry coulis.

## Ingredients
*(6 desserts, 18 cm diameter (7 in))*
### Rice mixture
300 g (10 oz) round (arborio) rice
1.5 L (6 cups) whole milk
1 vanilla bean
### Bavarian cream
1 L (1 qt) whole milk
1 vanilla bean
200 g (7 oz) egg yolks
300 g (10 oz) sugar
24 g (scant 1 oz) gelatin
600 ml (21/4 cups) heavy cream, whipped

### Glaze
500 g (1 lb) clear jelly glaze
250 g (8 oz) raspberry pulp
### Candied fruits
200 g (7 oz) candied fruits
100 ml (3.5 fl oz) Kirsch
### Flavored syrup
400 ml (14 fl oz) sugar syrup
400 ml (14 fl oz) crème de cassis
### Sponge cake
150 g (5 oz) egg yolks
185 g (6 oz) sugar
225 (7 1/2 oz) egg whites
185 g (6 oz) flour

# "Beethoven"

This pretty dessert is quick and easy to make and the ingredients are not too expensive (black currant purée may be found under its French name "purée de cassis" and can be replaced with red raspberry purée).

The colors liven up a display of desserts and the light, refreshing taste and texture make this an ideal dessert to serve after a copious meal.

## Ingredients

*(12 servings)*

2 sponge cake bands (for the sides)
2 sponge cake rounds (for the base)

### Black currant syrup

100 g (3 1/2 oz) black currant purée
100 g (3 1/2 oz) sugar syrup

### Apple Compote

5 firm, tart apples
1 vanilla bean
150 g (5 oz) sugar
100 g (3 1/2 oz) unsalted butter

### Black currant mousse

300 g (10 oz) black currant purée
90 g (3 oz) sugar
8 g (1/3 oz) gelatin
Few drops of Kirsch
300 ml (10 fl oz) heavy cream, whipped

### Black currant glaze

200 g (7oz) apple jelly
60 g (2 oz) black currant pureee
20 g (2/3 oz) glucose

## Procedure

### Apple compote

Peel, seed and slice the apples. Combine the apples and butter with the vanilla bean (split) in a heavy pan and cook over low heat about 15 minutes.

Add the sugar and cook a few more minutes. Spread the compote on a baking sheet to cool.

### Black currant mousse

Prepare the mousse just before assembling the dessert.

Simmer the black currant purée with the sugar. Off the heat, dissolve the softened gelatin in the hot liquid.

Cool a little then add the Kirsch.

Chill until thickened but not set. Whip the cream to firm peaks and gently fold in.

### Black currant glaze

Melt the jelly and glucose over low heat then stir in the fruit purée. Spread the warm glaze on the dessert.

## Assembly

Place the striped sponge cake around the sides of the mold.

Place the round of sponge cake in the bottom and moisten with the cassis syrup.

Fill the mold half way up with the cooled apple compote.

Fill the mold to the top with the black currant mousse, smooth the top and chill to set.

Decorate the top with slices of caramelized apples.

## Presentation

Place the dessert on the top right of the plate. Below the cake, place a sugar rose.

Pipe a little black currant glaze on the left hand side of the plate and finish the presentation with a swan cut from an apple.

# "Birmingham"

It is preferable to serve a dessert this rich and dark in color during the fall and winter months.

This classic combination of dark and white chocolate creates an uncomplicated and "clean" presentation.

Serve this dessert well chilled accompanied by a Banyuls or brut Champagne.

## Procedure

Prepare the almond sponge cake (whisk almond paste with eggs and sugar) and color a portion of the batter to make striped bands for the sides of the cakes.

Prepare the plain sponge cake for the base, pipe the batter in a 16 cm (13 1/4 in) (or in small circles for individual cakes) onto a parchment-lined baking sheet.

Prepare the dark chocolate mixture. Make the bombe mixture by beating the hot syrup into the egg yolks and beating until thick and cool. Add the melted chocolate and whipped cream. The white chocolate mixture is prepared the same way except that gelatin is carefully blended into the whipped cream. (See note)

*Note :* To incorporate the gelatin into the whipped cream, soften then melt the gelatin with a little water. Cool to room temperature. Stir in a little cream then fold this mixture into the whipped cream.

Important : This delicate procedure is difficult with a large quantity.

## Ingredients

*(5 desserts 18 cm 7 in) diameter*

### Almond sponge cake

500 g (1 lb) eggs
350 g (12 oz) egg whites
50 g (1/4 cup) sugar
750 g (1 1/2 lbs) almond paste
100 g (3 1/2 oz) flour
75 g (2 1/2 oz) melted unsalted butter

### Sponge cake (for the base)

100 g (3 1/2 oz) egg yolks
125 g (4 oz) sugar
150 g (5 oz) egg whites
125 g (4 oz) flour

### Cookie batter

*(for three sheets)*
100 g (3 1/2 oz) unsalted butter
100 g ( 3 1/2 oz) powdered sugar
100 g (3 1/2 oz) egg whites
70 g (2 1/3 oz) flour
30 g (1 oz) cocoa powder

### Dark chocolate mixture

75 g (2 1/2 oz) egg yolks
150 g (5 oz) sugar syrup
250 g (8 oz) dark covering chocolate
500 ml (2 cups) heavy cream, whipped

### White chocolate mixture

75 g (2 1/2 oz) egg yolks
150 g (5 oz) sugar syrup
250 g (8 oz) white covering chocolate
500 ml (2 cups) heavy cream, whipped
6 oz (1/6 oz)1 tsp gelatin

800 g (1 lb 10 oz) macerated sour cherries

### Syrup

400 ml (14 fl oz) sugar syrup
400 ml (14 fl oz) cherry juice

### Chocolate coating

250 g (8 oz) covering chocolate
250 g (8 oz) cocoa butter
Red food coloring

## Assembly

Cut the bands of striped almond sponge cake to cover the sides 3/4 of the way up. Place the round of plain sponge cake in the bottom and moisten with syrup.

Spread a layer of dark chocolate mousse, smooth the top and sprinkle the drained cherries over the surface.

Place the second layer of sponge cake on top and moisten with syrup.

Add a layer of white chocolate mousse to the top, smooth and chill until firm.

Spray the top with chocolate and heat the metal ring to remove it easily and neatly.

## Plate presentation

Place a portion of mousse cake on one third of the plate.

Place a chocolate "butterfly" dusted with cocoa to the side. On the remaining third of the plate, place three fresh cherries or a few macerated ones. Dust with cocoa.

Blend cherry syrup with jelly glaze and pipe a few drops on the plate.

# French Apple Crumb Tart

This French version of an American classic crumb-topped pie combines sweet with sour and crispy with soft and moist. It is best when eaten warm so that all the flavors combine well. The apple mixture can be replaced or combined with cooked rhubarb.

For a festive touch, accompany each slice of tart with vanilla ice cream and serve with Champagne.

## Ingredients

### Sweet pie pastry

50 g (5 oz) unsalted butter
100 g (3 1/2 oz) powdered sugar
100 g (3 1/2 oz) ground almonds
60 ml (2 fl oz) heavy cream
3 g (1/4 tsp) baking powder
200 g (7 oz) flour
5 g (1/2 tsp) cinnamon
Grated zest of 1/2 lemon

### Filling

2.4 kg (5 lbs) cooking apples
300 g (10 oz) unsalted butter
300 g (10 oz) sugar
Few drops of prune of apple brandy
Cinnamon to taste
200 g (7 oz) fresh raspberries

### Crumb topping

100 g (3 1/2 oz) unsalted butter
100 g (3 1/2 oz) light brown sugar
100 g (3 1/2 oz) flour
3 g (1/4 tsp) baking powder
50 g (1 2/3 oz) ground almonds

## Procedure

To make the pastry, cream the butter and sugar, then incorporate the remaining ingredients. Flatten into disks, refrigerate until firm. Roll out the dough to about 5 mm (1/6 in) and cut circles 18 cm (7 in) with a stainless steel ring. Chill the circle then bake at 180 C (360 F) in the metal forms until set but not too browned. Remove the forms, trim the edges with a sharp paring knife and replace the forms.

Make the apple filling; peel and cut the apples into thin slices. Cook over medium heat with butter and suagr until very soft.

Cover the bottom of the cooked pastry with raspberries cut in half. Spoon the apple filling over the raspberries in an even layer. Mix the ingredients for the topping into large crumbs and spread evenly over the top of the apples.

Place in a hot oven for a few minutes or under the broiler to brown the topping.

Remove the metal form and serve warm or cold. If selling this tart by the slice in a shop, press a piece of plastic wrap over the cut portion to keep the filling neat and to show off the raspberries inside.

## Assembly

Sweet pastry base
Layer of raspberries
Cooked apple filling
Crumb topping

## Plate presentation

Place a slice of the tart on one the side of the plate. Next to the tart, arrange a thick slice of cooked apple, a few raspberries and a fresh mint leaf.

On the remaining portion of the plate, place a scoop of raspberry sorbet or vanilla ice cream placed on a cookie.

Finish the presentation with a little raspberry sauce and some chocolate decorations.

# Hazelnut and Chocolate Mousse Cake

The successful marriage of coffee and chocolate is enhanced in this dessert with chopped hazelnuts in a crispy meringue and raisins macerated in Cognac.

This is a wonderful dessert to serve with a full flavored coffee.

## Procedure

### *Hazelnut dacquoise*

280 g (9 1/3 oz) hazelnuts
280 g (9 1/3 oz) sugar
25 g (3/4 oz) flour
300 g (10 oz) egg whites
50 g 1 2/3 oz) unsalted butter (melted, cooled)
5 g (1/16 oz) grated orange zest

Whisk the egg whites with 1/4 of the sugar until firm peaks are formed.

Mix the remaining sugar with the hazelnuts (1/2 chopped coarsely, 1/2 ground finely) and flour.

Fold the sugar mixture into the beaten egg whites then the melted butter.

On parchment paper-lined baking sheets, pipe 6 rounds of meringue 18 cm (7 in) in diameter using a large plain tip.

Bake at 220 C (425 F) about 20 minutes.

### *Chocolate mousse*

Bring the milk to a boil and pour over the chopped chocolate. When the chocolate has melted, stir until smooth and set aside to cool. When the ganache is cool but not not too firm, fold in the whipped cream.

Pipe 6 rounds of mousse 18 cm (7 in) in diameter on parchment paper. Cover and place in the freezer to become firm.

### *Raisins macerated in Cognac*

Cover the raisins with water, bring to a simmer and drain. Cover with Cognac and set aside to macerate for several days.

## Assembly

In the bottom of each ring mold, place a cardboard base and a circle of baked hazelnut meringue.

Spread a layer of freshly made coffee Bavarian on the bottom and sides of the mold.

Sprinkle macerated raisins over the Bavarian layer.

Place the frozen disks of chocolate mousse on top then spread the remaining Bavarian over the mousse. Smooth the top, cover and place in the freezer.

## Ingredients

### *Coffee Bavarian*

1 L (1 qt) whole milk - 250 g (8 oz) sugar
160 g (5 1/3 oz) egg yolks
100 g (3 1/2 oz) roasted coffee beans
10 g (2 tsp) instant coffee
30 g (1 oz) gelatin
1 L (1 qt) heavy cream, whipped

Grind the coffee beans coarsely. Heat the milk to a simmer, pour over the coffee, cool to room temperature then strain.

Whisk the egg yolks and sugar until thick and lemon-colored.

Heat the coffee-flavored milk to a simmer, pour a little into the egg yolks then return all of the ingredients to the saucepan. Cook over medium low heat, stirring constantly, until the custard coats the spoon. Dissolve the softened gelatin in the hot custard, strain then chill until cool and thickened but not completely set.
Gently fold in the whipped cream

### *Chocolate mousse*

400 g (14 oz) covering chocolate
250 ml (1 cup) whole milk
400 ml (14 fl oz) heavy cream

### *Macerated raisins*

600 g (1 lb 3 1/2 oz) raisins
200 ml (7 fl oz) Cognac

### Decoration

Drizzle chocolate glaze over the top then

brush with clear jelly glaze. Arrange kumquats and chocolate decorations on top.

## Plate presentation

Pipe some coffee crème anglaise around the plate. Place a portion of the desssert to one side and two chocolate fans on the other. Arrange slices of exotic fruits on the remainder of the plate.

# "Pêcher Mignon"

This is a refreshing chilled peach dessert to serve in the summer months. The touch of cinnamon adds just the right flavor to enhance the fruit.

This light cake is ideal for a tea room dessert cart. For restaurant service, the colors and combination of flavors will inspire beautiful plate presentations.

Although making the "chibouste" requires a certain level of skill, this is not a difficult dessert to prepare. The shelf life of this type of filling is limited.

The subtle peach flavor would go well with a sweet white wine or a "Kir royal à la pêche"- bubbling wine with a little peach brandy.

## Ingredients

For 3 desserts 18 X 4.5 cm (7 in X 1 3/4 in)

*Chocolate sponge cake*

75 g (12 1/2 oz) egg whites
480 g (1 lb) sugar
300 g (10 oz) egg yolks
150 g (5 oz) cocoa powder

*Caramelized peaches*

500 g (1 lb) peaches
50 g (1 2/3 oz) unsalted butter
30 g (1 oz) sugar

*Cinnamon chibouste*

500 ml (2 cups) whole milk
135 g (4 1/2 oz) egg yolks
60 g (2 oz) sugar
40 g (1 1 3/ oz) cornstarch
9 g (1/3 oz) gelatin
8 g (1 tsp) cinnamon
160 g (5 1/2 oz) egg whites
210 g (7 oz) sugar

*Peach aspic*

(250 g for each dessert)
75 g (12 1/2 oz) peach purée
75 g (2 1/2 oz) sugar
7 g (scant 1/3 oz) gelatin
225 g (7 3/4 oz) peaches, peeled, cut in cubes
50 g (1 2/3 oz) unsalted butter
40 g (1 1/3 oz) sugar

## Decoration

300 g (10 oz) covering chocolate

## Procedure

Prepare the flourless chocolate sponge cake batter and immediately pipe 6x16 cm (6 in) circles on baking sheets lined with parchment paper. Bake at 175 C (350 F) about 15 minutes.

Prepare the molded peach aspic. Cook peaches in butter and sugar, then purée. Incorporate the softened gelatin into the hot purée then the diced fruit. Pour the mixture into three 16 cm (6 in) ring molds set on parchment, chill to set.

Prepare the caramelized peach slices. Arrange the peach slices in a single layer on a parchment paper-lined baking sheet. Sprinkle generously with sugar and bake in a hot oven or under the broiler. If cooked in a pan on the stovetop, the peaches may break apart.

## Assembly

Place circles of chocolate sponge cake in the base of three ring molds 18 X 4.5 cm (7 X 1 3/4 in).

The sides can be lined with striped cake.

Prepare the peach chibouste and spread about 1/9 of the mixture in each mold.

Carefuly place the molded peach aspic on top of the chibouste layer.

Spread a thin layer of chibouste over the aspic.

Arrange the caramelized peach slices on top of the chibouste.

Place a second layer of sponge cake on top then spread the remaining chibouste over the cake and spread it to the edges with a spatula and smooth the top.

Place in the refrigerator or freezer to set the chibouste.

Sprinkle the top with sugar and place under the broiler a few seconds to caramelize.

## Decoration

Decorate the top with a few peach slices and chocolate cigarettes.

## Plate presentation

Place a slice of the dessert (already decorated) near the rim of a large dinner plate.

Fan out some peach slices on the other side of the plate. Add a few red berries and a mint leaf for color.

Add a peach sauce to the plate accented with a few drops of raspberry sauce for contrast.

More peach slices can be added if needed. Finish the decoration with a few chocolate cigarettes which look like the rolled bark of the cinnamon tree.

# Strawberry Cake

The classic French "Fraisier" is made with plain genoise. Here the sponge cake is flavored with hazelnuts and almonds which enhance the taste of the strawberries.

This dessert is not difficult to make. The mousseline filling is lower in fat and sugar than many other creamy mixtures.

Once assembled, this cake will keep only 24 hours in the refrigerator.

## Ingredients

Hazelnut and almond cake (2 cakes 40 X 60 cm 16 X 24 in)

500 g (1 lb) ground hazelnuts
500 g (1 lb) ground almonds
1 kilo (2.2 lbs) sugar
1.2 K (2 1/2 lbs) egg whites
200 g (7 oz) butter

### Mousseline

1 L (1 qt) whole milk
160 g (5 1/3 oz) egg yolks (8)
60 g (2 oz) flour
70 g (2 1/3 oz) cornstarch
500 g (1 lb) unsalted butter
250 g ( 8 oz) sugar
200 ml (7 fl oz) heavy cream

### Clear glaze

1.8 L (7 1/2 cups) water
200 g (1 cup) sugar
40 g (1/3 oz) pectin
40 drops citric acid
190 g (scant 1 cup) sugar
750 g (1 1/2 lbs) glucose

## Procedure

### Nut cake

Beat the egg whites to firm peaks and beat in the sugar to "tighten" them.
Fold in the ground nuts and the butter (melted and cooled).
Bake at 200 C (400 F) about 30 minutes.
Store baked cakes in the refrigerator.

### Mousseline

Prepare a pastry cream with the sugar, egg yolks, flour and cornstarch.
Cool to room temperature. Beat in the butter until light and smooth, then fold in the whipped cream.

### Chocolate covering

The "basket" marks on the cake are made by spraying liquid chocolate through a stencil with that pattern.
Carefully brush clear glaze over the dessert.

## Plate presentation

Place a doily on the plate and arrange a portion of the cake to one side.

On the other side of the plate, place a cone made of decorated almond paste or white chocolate with stawberries and raspberries.

# Tropical "Milles Feuilles"

This "Napoleon" or "milles feuilles" as the French call it (named for the "thousand leaves" in the pastry) uses the exciting taste of passion fruit in the chibouste filling.

The fragile pastry will not stay crisp very long, so it must be eaten the day that it is made. Take care when cutting the various elements so that they will stack neatly.

This is a wonderful dessert to enjoy in the summer with a glass of pink Champagne.

## Ingredients

### Passion fruit chibouste

250 ml (1 cup) passion fruit pulp
100 g (3 1/2 oz (1/2 cup))sugar
4 egg yolks
30 g (1 oz) cornstarch
4 egg whites (with 20 g (2/3 oz) sugar)
6 g (1/6 oz) gelatin

### Puff pastry

250 g (8 oz) flour
7 g (1 1/2 tsp) salt
125 ml (1/2 cup) water
250 g (8 oz) unsalted butter with
100 g (3 1/2 oz) flour
Raspberry aspic
250 ml (1 cup) raspberry pulp
50 g (1/4 cup) sugar
6 g (1/6 oz) gelatin, softened

## Procedure

### Passion fruit chibouste

Prepare the chibouste just before assembling the dessert. Whisk together the sugar and egg yolks until thick and lemon-colored.

Mix the cornstarch into the egg yolks, then the passion fruit pulp. In a non reactive pot, cook this mixture over medium low heat, whisking contantly until it thickens.

Remove the cooked mixture from the heat, stir in the softened gelatin.

Beat the egg whites to stiff peaks, adding the sugar a little at a time towards the end to "tighten" the texture of the meringue. Fold the warm custard into the meringue.

### Puff pastry

Mix the water and salt into the flour to make a dough. Cover and place in the refrigerator for about 15 minutes to relax the gluten.

Mix the 100 g (3 1/2 oz) of flour into the butter, form into a rectangle, cover and chill for about 30 minutes. Roll out the dough into a rectangle twice the size of the butter. Place the butter on one half and fold the dough over it to form a package with a layer of butter in the center, seal the edges. Roll out to a rectangle. Fold into

thirds. Roll out into a longer rectangle then fold into fourths (both ends into the middle, then fold like a book). Rest the dough 20 minutes, repeat the same rolling prodecure, rest the dough again before shaping.

Roll the dough into 2 sheets 20 X 30 cm (8 X 12 in), prick all over with a fork and chill for 30 minutes before baking.

Bake in a preheated 210-220 C (400-425 F) oven, about 20 minutes or until evenly browned.

Sprinkle powdered sugar on the cooked pastry and return to a hot oven to caramelize the sugar. Set aside to cool.

### Passion fruit aspic

Soften the gelatin in cold juice or water. (If using gelatin sheets, soften in cold water.) Heat the passion fruit pulp to a simmer and stir in the softened gelatin. Add the sugar, stir to dissolve. Pour the mixture into a non reactive pan 16 X 22 X 1 cm (6 X 9 X 3/8 in).

Chill until firm in the refrigerator of freezer.

## Assembly

Spread about half of the chibouste in an even layer on one of the puff pastry sheets.

Place in the freezer about 15 minutes to set up. Unmold the sheet of aspic and place it on top of the firm chibouste.

Spread the remaining chibouste over the aspic then place the second sheet of pastry on top. Cover and place in the freezer until firm. Cut in rectangles, squares or rounds with a serrated knife.

Brush the top with a clear jelly glaze and decorate with some passion fruit seeds.

## Plate presentation

On one third of the plate, make an arrangement of several exotic fruits like star fruit, lychee, kumquat and passion fruit.

Place a portion of "milles feuilles" to one side.

Complete the presentation with passoin fruit sauce piped in a decorative design.

# "Cinnamon Tree"

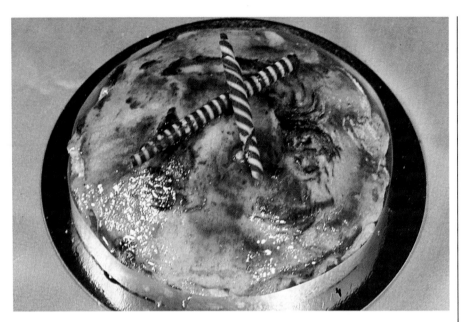

This dessert is lovely to look at as well as a pleasure to eat. The combination of caramel and cinnamon is very appetizing and would be an appropriate dessert after any meal in any season.

The chibouste and caramel custard require attention to detail to achieve the desired reulats. The dessert can be kept frozen but the caramel cage must be added the day it is served.

## Ingredients

*(Yields 4 desserts 18 X 4.5 cm (7 X 2 in))*

### Hazelnut dacquoise

400 g (14 oz) egg whites
320 g (11 oz) sugar
240 g (6 oz) ground hazelnuts
80 g (2 2/3 oz) ground almonds
160 g (5 1/3 oz) powdered sugar

*Note :* Bake this dacquoise in two stages, first at 230 C (450 F) a few minutes then lower to 200 C (400 F) for about 50 minutes.

### Cointreau syrup

100 ml (3.5 fl oz) sugar syrup
50 ml (scant 2 fl oz) Cointreau
1 tsp peach brandy

## Assembly

Place the dacquise in the bottom of the form and pour the caramel on top. Place the meringue on top then spread the cinnamon chibouste over the top and smooth with a spatula.

## Plate presentation

The base for the dessert is a circle of striped almond sponge cake slightly larger than the molded chibouste. Also cut three half moon shapes of cake per dessert. Place the unmolded chibouste on the cake and place it on one side of the plate. On the other side place a caramel cage and fan out the half moon-shaped cakes. Sprinkle a little ground cinnamon over one side of the plate.

### Caramel cream

250 ml (1 cup) heavy cream
1/2 vanilla bean
250 g (8 oz) caramel (see below)
100 g (3 1/2 oz) egg yolks
Italian meringue (60 g (2 oz) egg whites + 90 g (3 oz) sugar
750 ml (3 cups) heavy cream, whipped
8 g (scant 1/3 oz) gelatin

### Cinnamon chibouste

120 ml (scant 1/2 cup) heavy cream
60 ml (2 fl oz) whole milk
1/2 vanilla bean
100 g (3 1/2 oz) egg yolks
100 g (3 1/2 oz) sugar
12 g (scant 1/2 oz) cornstarch
9 g (1/3 oz) gelatin
2.5 g (1/2 tsp) ground cinnamon
145 g (5 oz) egg whites

### Caramel

500 g (1 lb) sugar
330 ml (11 fl oz) heavy cream, whipped

### Italian meringue

200 g (7 oz) egg whites
300 g (10 oz) sugar
100 ml (3.5 fl oz) water

# "Quatre Epices"

"Quatre epices" is a blend of cloves, ginger, white pepper and nutmeg. Cinnamon is also used for this preparation. In France the spice blend is sold already ground and mixed. These intense flavors enhance the chocolate and almonds in the dessert.

If prepared with great care the mousse and glaze in this desssert freeze very well.

## Ingredients

### Spice genoise

300 g (10 oz) egg yolks
435 g (15 oz) whole eggs
600 g (3 cups) sugar
150 g (5 oz) cornstarch
75 g (2 1/2 oz) egg yolks
75 g (2 1/2 oz) cocoa powder
5 g (1 tsp) spice blend (see below
15 g (1/2 oz) baking powder

### Spice blend

Blend equal amounts cinnamon and "quatre epices"

### Chocolate praline mousse

375 g (12 1/2 oz) egg yolks
300 g (10 oz) sugar, cooked to 120 C (250 F)
9 g (1/3 oz) gelatin
750 g (1 1/2 lbs) dark covering chocolate
375 g (12 1/2 oz) praline paste
1.5 L (6 cups) heavy cream, whipped

### Caramelized almonds

500 g (1 lb) unblanched almonds
200 g (1 cup) sugar
1 tsp "quatre epices"
1 tsp butter

### Chocolate glaze

("restaurant" proportions)

1.7 L (7 cups) whole milk
1.3 L (5 1/2 cups) heavy cream
1.7 L (7 cups) sugar syrup
600 g (1 lb 3 12/ oz) glucose
1.3 kilos (2.75 lbs) covering chocolate
4 kilos (8.75 lbs) fondant
Red food coloring as needed

## Procedure

### Genoise

Beat 300 g (10 oz) egg yolks, the eggs and sugar until thick and lemon-colored.

Sift together the cornstarch, cocoa, spices and baking powder and fold gently into the egg yolk mixture.

Spread the batter on 2 parchment-lined baking sheets and bake at 230 C (450 F).

### Chocolate praline mousse

Make a bombe mixture. Soften the gelatin and dissolve in the bombe mixture while it is still hot.

Melt the chocolate and heat to 45 C (125 F) then cool to room temperature, gently fold into the whipped cream.

Stir a little bombe mixture into the praline paste to lighten it then blend all the praline into the bombe mixture.

Gently stir together the two mixtures. Place into a mold with the genoise base, chill to firm. Decorate with almonds.

### Plate presentation

Cover the bottom of the plate with caramel. Place a portion of the dessert in the center or off to one side.

Just before serving sprinkle a little cocoa powder over the dessert.

# "Arpajon"

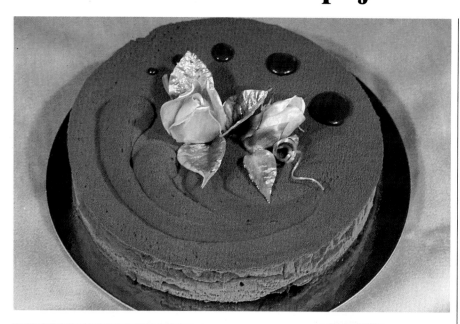

This stunning dessert won the top honors for renowned pastry chef Lucien Peltier. It combines a deep chocolate mousse with a vanilla crème brulée. The almond sponge cake adds a wonderful flavor.

The Arpajon is not difficult to make nor is it very expensive. It also keeps well in the freezer, making it an ideal choice for home cooks as well as pastry shop owners and restauranteurs.

## Ingredients

*For 5 desserts 18 X 4 cm (7 X 1 1/2 in)*

### Chocolate mousse

*Bombe mixture :*

285 g (9 1/2 oz) egg yolks
375 g (12 1/2 oz) sugar syrup

*Chocolate mixture :*

1.55 L (6 1/4 cups) heavy cream, whipped
750 g (1 1/2 lbs) dark covering chocolate

### Vanilla crème brulée

500 ml (2 cups) whole milk
500 ml (2 cups) heavy cream
180 g (6 oz) sugar
320 g (10 2/3 oz) egg yolks
4 g (1/6 oz) gelatin

### Sponge cake

*(2 sheets, 40 X 60 cm (16 X 24 in))*

10 eggs
500 g (1 lb) sugar
200 g (7 oz) ground almonds
300 g (10 oz) flour
500 g (1 lb) unsalted butter

## Plate presentation

Place the dessert to one side of the plate and fill the other side with caramelized "crème brulée" and a sprinkling of cocoa powder.

## Procedure

### Chcolate mousse

Make the bombe mixture with the egg yolks and sugar syrup.
Fold the cooled, melted chocolate into the whipped cream.
Fold together the two mixtures.

### Crème brulée

Blend all the ingredients pour into the mold.
Bake at 100 C (225 F) until set. Cool to room temperature then freeze.

### Sponge cake

Prepare the batter and bake at 200 C (400 F) for 10-15 minutes.

## Assembly

Use stainless steel rings to assemble the dessert. Place a cardboard base in the bottom then a round of sponge cake cut slightly smaller than the ring.
Unmold the frozen crème and place it on top of the cake. Trim the crème layer if necessary to leave a little room at the top for a thin layer of mouse.
Spread mousse over the top and down the sides to cover completely.
Smooth the top, cover and store in the freezer.

# "Frou-Frou"

This rich dessert is best served in the fall and winter and the portions should be small. Attention should be paid to the temperature and consistency of the chocolate while making the rich, caramel-based mousse, but otherwise the preparation is not difficult.

## Ingredients

*(12 servings)*
1 round of hazelnut meringue
200 g (7 oz) toasted, chopped hazelnuts

### Chocolate mousse

100 g (3 1/2 oz) egg yolks
100 g (3 1/2 oz or 1/2 cup) sugar
200 g (7 oz) covering chocolate
500 ml (2 cups) heavy cream

### Chocolate praline layer

200 g (7 oz) praline paste
100 g (3 1/2 oz) covering chocolate
60 g (2 oz) chopped toffee or crisp cookies)

### Shiny chocolate glaze

00 g (3 1/2 oz) cocoa butter
100 g (3 1/2 oz) covering chocolate
Few drops red food coloring

## Procedure

### Chocolate praline layer

Temper the covering chocolate to 40 C (98 F). Blend the melted chocolate with the praline and chopped cookies then spread on a parchment-lined baking sheet.
Cover with plastic wrap. Place in the freezer to firm.

### Chocolate mousse

The base of this chocolate mousse is a caramel bombe mixture. Cook the sugar to a light caramel then reduce the temperature to 118 C (250 F) before beating the sugar syrup into the egg yolks. Continue to beat at medium speed until the mixture is thick and cooled.
Melt the chocolate to 50 C (130 F), cool. Beat the cream to firm peaks.
Gently fold the melted chocolate then the whipped cream into the cooled bombe mixture.

## Assembly

Assemble in a large metal ring or individual spherical molds. Place a base of sponge cake in the bottom and sprinkle toasted, chopped hazelnuts over the cake.
Pipe mousse mixture to come about halfway up the mold.

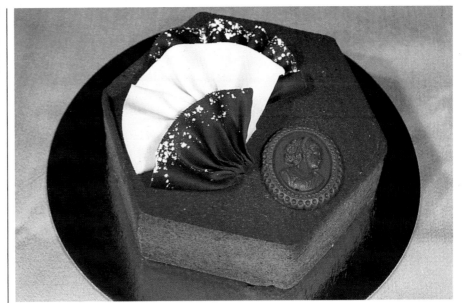

Cut the pastry a little smaller than the mold and place on top of the mousse. Pipe mousse to the top and smooth with a spatula.
Cover and place in the freezer.

### Chocolate coating

Melt the chocolate and cocoa butter to 50 C (130 F), add a few drops of red food coloring. Use a pastry gun to spray the chocolate coating over the well chilled dessert.

## Plate presentation

Place the dessert (either a portion of the larger cake or an individual serving) in the center of the left hand side of the plate.
On the top right hand side place three chocolate fans sprinkled with powdered sugar.
Below the chocolate fans, place the medallion of chocolate on the tear-shaped disk of almond paste.

# Presentation pieces at the Charles Proust competition

## A Display of Talent and Creativity

*Each year, Saint-Michel (a French organization for pastry chefs) holds a competition called the Charles Proust, for professional chefs and young pastry chefs (junior class), in which they present artistic presentation pieces based on a theme. The theme changes every year; the pieces shown here are organized around the theme of provinces of France.*

*The following pages show exhibition pieces that exemplify use of the many techniques possible in pastry making, including various doughs, creams, and batters. Confections, sugar work, chocolate work, and modeling can all be seen.*

*All the techniques used in the presentation pieces have been explained in the four volumes of this series.*

*The Saint-Michel society was formed in 1868 and is made up of pastry chefs and pastry shop proprietors. The group works together to grade and judge the contestants. Saint-Michel has contributed to the development of pastry making and support of pastry chefs at all levels, in France and throughout the world.*

*At lower left: the three techniques for writing and decorating with a paper cone can be seen here. The two pieces on the left were made using the applied technique; the center pieces, using the sliding technique; and the right two pieces, using the thread technique.*

**Place Charles-Proust
By O. LUCEL**

# L'Auvergne

**J. P. ETIENVRE**

This piece won first prize at the Charles Proust Competition and clearly displays the importance of art in the field of pastry making.

Pastillage was used for a great deal of the work. Note how it shines and gives the effect of lacquered wood. The detail and respect for proportion are striking. This is an excellent example of how pastillage can be used to represent objects realistically.

The photographs on these two pages show the use of several techniques for applying color: a paintbrush was used to paint the butterfly; an atomizer, for shadowing the pastillage flowers; the pulled-sugar flowers and leaves were colored before being shaped.

The strings of cotton were made with royal icing piped from a paper cone.

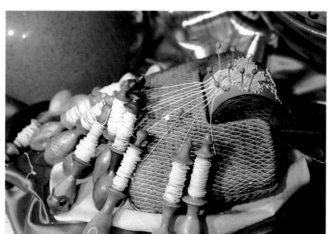

# Le Nord

## P. HOURDEQUIN

The tiers in this piece were made of pastillage and decorated with royal icing. The molded columns were most likely made from pastillage or turned sugar. The figures were made from blown sugar. Objects were attached together either by using pulled sugar or by heating their extremities. Attaching pieces with sugar is difficult, and the effort is sometimes visible in this piece.

Note the detail given to the hands, which were made from pulled sugar. The fingers were carefully cut with a scissors to separate them without making them overly fragile.

The cake represents an overturned copper bowl and is covered with a golden yellow glaze. The glaze was caramelized on the sides and slightly burned on the bottom to give the effect of a real copper bowl used for cooking candies.

# *Flandres-Artois*

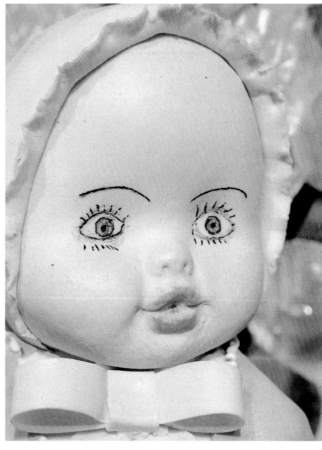

### C. CNOCKAERT

The foliage made from pulled sugar was colored and shadowed with an airbrush to create the impression of a sunbeam shining on the piece. The face of the doll was molded from pastillage, and a sheet of pastillage was used to form the bonnet that covers her head. The pastillage was colored before it was shaped; the whites of the eyes were carefully painted.

Great care and attention were given to making the hands of the doll, a very difficult procedure.

The cherries on the cake are highlighted by and match the color of the flowers.

# Les Ardennes

**E. SAGUEZ**

This piece is interesting as much for the ambience it creates as for the way it was made.

The head of the wild boar was made mostly of pastillage, as was the support to which it is attached. The head is well proportioned and colored.

The painting gives a sense of depth to the piece. The flowers and petals were made from pulled sugar and have a beautiful satin finish.

The cake has a velvetlike texture created by using a paint spray gun filled with chocolate. The cake was frozen before it was sprayed, as it had to be very cold for this procedure.

# La Champagne

**M. RAINAUD**

The famous cathedral in Reims is represented here, placed inside a barrel used for Champagne. Both were made from pastillage and royal icing.

There is a great deal of sugar work in this piece: blown sugar in the bunches of grapes and pulled-sugar flowers and leaves. A paper cone was used for detail work on the cathedral and the writing on the cake. The cork was made out of pastillage and colored before being shaped.

# L'Alsace

### L. GUILLET

This composition marries sugar work with chocolate work in matching tones. The painting made from cocoa ties the piece together. The velvet texture given to the cake was obtained by using a paint spray gun filled with a mixture of unsweetened or couverture chocolate and cocoa butter.

Note the neat, realistic writing on the wine label, made with a paintbrush and finished by scraping it clean with a knife.

# L'Alsace

**Y. KOBARI**

This piece catches the eye with its bright colors. The painting, made with food coloring, seems to be waiting for the first ray of sunshine, which has already brightened the pulled-sugar leaves.

The kouglof mold was decorated with a paper cone and painted with a brush.

The evergreen branch was made of gummed royal icing.

The pine cone was made of pastillage and colored with either a paintbrush or a sponge.

# L'Alsace

**S. KATUHITO**

Each object in this presentation piece was carefully proportioned and placed in such a way as to give the entire piece a sense of depth.

The side of the cake consists of small squares made from layers of sponge cake and preserves. Creating it required a great deal of work, rarely seen in pastry shops because it is extremely time consuming.

The stork is made from blown and pulled sugar. The ribbon, leaves, and rose demonstrate a fine skill in working with pulled sugar. The Alsatian house is very cleanly and neatly assembled, not an easy feat to accomplish.

# *La Bourgogne*

**N. CHARRIER (junior competition)**

This is a very complex piece, an excellent example of a situation in which each element must fit exactly in place, requiring precise calculations.

The roof and base were painted by hand with a brush, which is very exacting work.

The writing on the cake was done with the applied technique using a paper cone filled with royal icing.

This contestant obviously researched the Gothic writing style. The design also includes a grape vine and caricature of Bacchus, the Roman god of wine.

247

# La Bourgogne

**J. URGEGHE (junior competition)**

This piece won the first prize in the junior competition. The contrast between the bright and fresh look of the bouquet of flowers and leaves made from pulled sugar and the darkness of the blacksmith's shop is striking and well balanced. Unusually fine detail was given to small articles.

# Le Lyonnais

**A. ROLANCY**

This piece is centered primarily around autumn foliage made from pulled sugar. The various leaf colors were obtained by coloring the sugar before it was pulled rather than coloring the leaves after they were shaped.

The flowers were made by attaching pulled-sugar petals to a small ball of blown sugar, creating an imaginary, though beautiful, flower.

The painting, made using a paper cone filled with decorating chocolate, displays artistic talent.

# La Savoie

**B. LEGER (junior competition)**

Based on the theme of a "little Savoyard chimneysweep," this piece is particularly interesting for the way articles were colored.

The ski, most likely made from pastillage, is especially well painted to resemble a wooden ski.

# L'Ardèche

**S. BILLET**

The highlight of this piece is the beautiful bird of paradise set in a bouquet of pulled-sugar flowers and leaves. Blown sugar was used to make the body of the bird, and poured sugar for the tail, which is attached to metal rods covered with pulled sugar.

# Le Périgord

**D. LEBIGRE**

Although not difficult to produce, it is unusual to see the type of sugar work that forms the back of this piece and the piece on the following page, which are both made from rock sugar.

The ancient rock paintings in the caves of Lascaux, made by prehistoric man, are represented here by two different competitors on these two pages. Lebigre painted the rock sugar with a sponge and brush, while Guerre used an airbrush and molded the rock sugar on a sheet pan, giving it a smooth surface.

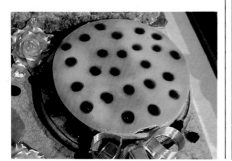

# Le Périgord

**R. GUERRE**

The top of this cake was decorated with a special tool normally used for painting on wood. This technique must be done on a firm surface; freezing the cake is the best way to accomplish this.

Note the detail in the fruit and its accurate proportion. The colors in the fruit and pulled-sugar flowers brighten this piece.

# *Les Pyrénées*

**Ch. PUBILL**

This piece is an excellent example of the use of harmonious colors. The colors in the painting are reinforced by the bouquet of pulled-sugar flowers and leaves. The butterflies were made from pastillage and painted with a brush after being assembled.

The frame and painting, of pastillage, were probably made separately and later attached together. The Pyrénées figurine was made of blown and pulled sugar.

# Les Pyrénées

**D. LEMEUR**

These two somewhat austere pieces are most striking for their beautiful, clean work with an airbrush, which was used to create the painting, the map, and shadows.

**G. TERRON**
**(junior competition)**

# Le Pays Basque

**Ch. LEMOY**

The bust was sculpted from fondant chocolate and covered with tempered couverture chocolate. The coating of couverture brightens the piece, making it more attractive than plain carved chocolate.

Notice the fine lines in the painting. As discussed in the section on painting in this volume (pages 64 to 65), the principal lines may have been made by tracing over a sheet covered with cocoa powder, placed on top of a firm background.

The decoration on the cake was made with a pastry bag and Saint-Honoré tip.

# Le Pays Basque

**F. GERNEZ**

**J.-P. LESBATS**

These two very different presentations are based on the same idea, the sport jai alai, popular in the Basque region. The piece on the left is surrounded by a large bouquet of pulled-sugar spring flowers and leaves of various colors. The piece on the right uses colors of the same tone. The player is caught in motion, ready to hit the ball. The *cestas* (wicker baskets) are both remarkably well reproduced, especially with regard to the weaving.

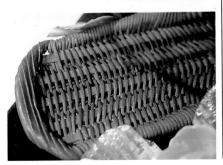

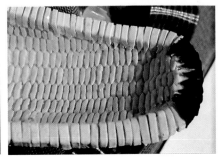

# *Les Charentes*

**D. BERNARD**

The cake in this piece was decorated with a paper cone filled with chocolate in the same color as the cake itself. The side of the cake reveals its composition and gives it a rather rustic appeal.

The bottle of Cognac was made from blown sugar.

The label on the bottle is most likely made from marzipan or a type of pastillage (called Japanese pastillage).

The label was probably placed on the bottle after being decorated, as it is easier to write on a flat surface.

# Les Charentes

**Ph. SIBILEAU**

The velvet texture of the cake was produced by using a paint sprayer filled with chocolate. The chocolate ribbon was made by spreading melted chocolate on a very cold sheet pan and lifting the chocolate as it set. The white lines were made by piping white chocolate over the dark chocolate, using a paper cone, before shaping the ribbon.

The Gothic-style writing on the painting was done with a brush cut at an angle.

# La Bretagne

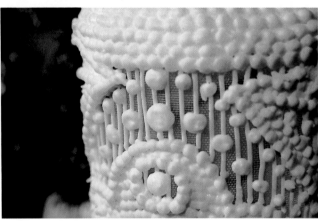

### A. VILLIERS

The Breton headdress was made entirely of royal icing, exacting work that is quite difficult. Using a tube as a support, royal icing was piped from a paper cone, line by line, to duplicate the various motifs of the lace in the headdress.

The thistles were made from pulled sugar and attached to a ball with a wire in the center, forming the stem.

The cake is presented on a crêpe skillet made from pastillage.

# La Bretagne

## J. PEDRO

Lavish foliage made from pulled sugar forms the background of this piece. The frame of the painting is made of royal icing piped from a pastry bag with a closely fluted tip.

Note how clean and exact the Gothic

## J. P. PANDOLFI

writing on the plate is; this was accomplished by using a paintbrush and paper cone.

# La Normandie

**V. DALLET**

The many iridescent objects in this piece seem to be illuminated by the sun. The apples, made from blown sugar, are set in a container, made from pastillage, that represents the containers used for Camembert cheese. Camembert is one of the most popular cheeses from the Normandy region. A boat is placed at the base of a flowering apple tree.

# La Normandie

### F. TOUAH (junior competition)

The apple press (Normandy is well known for its cider) was made from pastillage. The apples were made from blown sugar. The coat of arms was decorated with a paper cone and painted with a brush.

The ribbon on the cake and flowering apple branches were made from pulled sugar.

### C. MARIE

A container for Camembert cheese, made from pastillage, is used to hold the cake. The sculpture was carved from pale yellow-colored chocolate to resemble butter, butter being a specialty of the Normandy region.

# La Normandie

**J. M. LOUVARD (junior competition)**

The half-timbering on the Normandy-style house and the thatched roof were all made from pastillage. The pulled-sugar apples are set in a dish made from pastillage that was molded over a stainless steel plate. The molded plate was painted and then decorated with a paper cone.

# La Normandie

**F. VANDECAPELLE (junior competition)**

The two pieces on this page were based on classic arrangements and make good use of matching tones in the pulled-sugar flowers and blown-sugar fruits.

**M. PINEAU**

265

# *Le Val de Loire*

**K. TSUSHIYA**

The two contestants on this page make use of painting on pastillage, each using a very different style.

The perspective in both paintings is equally well respected. The walls of the château, made from pastillage and attached together with royal icing, were excellently colored so as to give the impression of old stone.

**M. BERTHOLD**

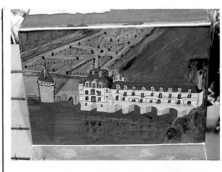

# La Beauce

## C. MARQUANT

The framed painting and its easel were both made from pastillage. The spikes of wheat were made from pulled sugar, each individual grain pulled separately and attached on a wire strand covered with pulled sugar. The ear of corn was made by molding blown sugar and was colored in successive layers with a sponge. The husk of corn was made from pulled sugar and attached at the base.

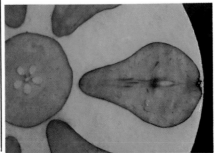

# L'Ile-de-France

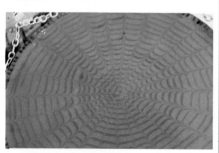

**O. LUCEL**

Made primarily from pastillage, this piece was probably first designed with scale drawings as this type of work requires very precise dimensions. The fronts and sides of the buildings were made separately, allowed to dry, and then attached together with royal icing.

Each structure could have been colored either by adding coloring to the pastillage before it was shaped or by painting the surface with a brush or sponge after the buildings were constructed.

Templates were used to gauge the sizes of the buildings before they were put together. The windows and corners were decorated with royal icing piped from a paper cone.

# Translators' Notes

Because these volumes were originally written for a French audience, some changes had to be made in the instructions to make them applicable to American practice. The following notes explain changes that were made, as well as some of the ingredients used in the recipes.

*Butter and shortening:* Most recipes call for butter because of its superior flavor. Other shortenings may be substituted in part or entirely, according to taste.

*Chocolate:* The French government strictly controls the quality and appelations of chocolate. The percentage of cocoa butter, cocoa liquor, and sugar are closely controlled. In France, there are various types and qualities of chocolate, which are discussed in detail in volume 3 of this series. Couverture chocolates (the better-quality chocolates) are made with a minimum of 31 percent cocoa butter; no other fats are allowed.

In the United States, what is referred to in this series as white chocolate is actually called white or confectionary coating, as it contains no chocolate, only cocoa butter, sugar, lecithin, and vanilla or other flavoring.

*Crème fraîche:* Recipes in this series often include crème fraîche. Crème fraîche is thicker than heavy cream but contains the same amount of butter fat. For most recipes, heavy cream can be substituted for crème fraîche.

*Flour:* Two types of flour are primarily used in the recipes in this series. In general, when products are to be light, such as cake batters, pure cake flour (without baking powder) is called for. When a batter requires more body, all-purpose flour is used. Breads usually require a strong, high-gluten flour, commonly called bread or patent flour. Many of the recipes requiring flour have been tested in the United States by the translators and have been proven to work. As the qualities of flours, as well as the conditions under which they are used (such as humidity and altitude) vary throughout the United States, the amount specified in a recipe may need to be adjusted slightly.

*French products:* As this series is based on French pastry-making practices, some of the products in it may be unfamiliar. All the products mentioned are available in the United States. Substitutes are given for products that may be difficult to find. All the French products (such as chocolate) can be obtained through wholesale companies that import such products.

*Gelatin:* In France, gelatin is marketed in 2-gram sheets, whereas in the United States, it is also sold in powdered form. Gelatin sheets vary in weight in the United States, so it is important to weigh them. The equivalent weight of powdered gelatin can be used to replace the gelatin sheets called for in the recipes. Gelatin sheets should always be softened before using them in a recipe by soaking them in cold water for several minutes and then squeezing them to remove the excess water.

*Measurements:* French professional pastry chefs customarily weigh their ingredients. For this reason, volume measurements are used only for liquids; dry ingredients are difficult to measure accurately by volume. Both metric and U.S. units of measure are given in the text. It is recommended that those who are serious about the profession of pastry making familiarize themselves with the metric system. Because metric measurement is based on units of ten, it is more accurate and easier to use. The metric system is also the most widely used system of measurement, standard almost everywhere but the United States.

Most U.S. conversions have been rounded off to the nearest half unit of measure, except for smaller quantities, when accuracy was important. Quantities less than 15 grams (½ ounce) are given in teaspoons and tablespoons.

*Pastry tips:* Pastry tip sizes are always indicated by a number. Unfortunately, each manufacturer numbers its tips differently. In this series, the pastry tip numbers are those most commonly used in France. These numbers often correspond to the diameter of the tip in millimeters. French pastry tips are available in the United States.

*Sheet pans:* Yields given in this series are based on the use of French equipment of standard dimensions. Professional-quality French sheet pans measure 40 x 60 cm (16 x 24 in.) and are made of heavy blue steel. It is always preferable to use the heaviest sheet pans available. If using different-sized sheet pans, be sure to take this into consideration when calculating the number of pastries to place on a pan.

*Sugars:* Various types of sugars are used in French pastry, each serving a different purpose. Use granulated sugar when no other indication is given.

Confectioners' sugar is sugar that has been finely ground into a powder. It often contains approximately 3 percent cornstarch to prevent caking.

Glucose, also called dextrose, is used along with granulated or cubed sugar when cooking sugar to prevent crystallization. It is also often used for sugar work such as pulled sugar or blown sugar. Corn syrup can be substituted for glucose in the recipes. It is somewhat lighter, however, and so more of it may be required.

Invert sugar, also called trimoline, is 25 to 30 percent sweeter than granulated sugar. It is made by breaking down sucrose into its components, glucose and fructose. Trimoline helps baked goods stay fresher longer because it holds moisture better than granulated sugar does. It is also used in sorbets, as it imparts a smoother texture than granulated sugar alone. Honey is an invert sugar and can be substituted for trimoline in small quantities. Of course, honey is not neutral in flavor, as trimoline is, and can impart an unwanted flavor to the product.

*Yeast:* The yeast called for in this series is always compressed fresh yeast, not the dry variety. If dry yeast must be substituted, it must be activated at a somewhat higher temperature than fresh yeast. Activate the dry yeast by first moistening it with 43° C (110° F) water. When substituting dry yeast for fresh, use 10 grams or 2 teaspoons of dry yeast for every 20 grams or 2/3 ounce of fresh yeast specified.

# Forewords

The *Professional French Pastry Series* consists of four volumes that I would have liked to have owned when I began my training as a professional pastry chef. Now that they are available, they are a resource that I will refer to often. These books are the first available to the serious pastry chef that contain clear and easy-to-follow instructions, which apprentice bakers will also appreciate.

To become a master pastry chef, you need a fine hand, patience, and knowledge. It takes a lot of hard work and perserverance, but the results are well worth the effort. These books show you how to prepare fine pastries using classical methods while allowing the freedom to develop your own ideas, styles, and techniques. Each volume builds upon the skills mastered in the preceding volumes; methods and recipes serve as a continuous source of ideas.

The art of French pastry making is like any art—it is done out of love. Achievements such as the publication of this series help bring respect to pastry making by demonstrating the seriousness of the technique. That's what I particularly like about these volumes—they take you through a precise body of knowledge, step by step, and build your appreciation for it.

I have always hoped that a reference like the *Professional French Pastry Series* would become available to the English-speaking pastry chef as a source to rely on during his or her day-to-day activities. These volumes carefully explain the chemistry of pastry making and include detailed timetables for the recipes. The volumes cover virtually every detail you would need to know in order to learn classical French pastry making. Until now, the only sources available were either in another language or were large collections of recipes without explanations of the methods and techniques. The experience and knowledge of the authors, Roland Bilheux and Alain Escoffier, are apparent throughout all four volumes. The fine abilities of the translators, Rhona Poritzky-Lauvand and Jim Peterson, are also evident.

No one volume or series of volumes can ensure the success of a professional pastry chef. A good resource, however, can help one to develop both the technical and the creative abilities needed for a successful career as a pastry chef. The *Professional French Pastry Series* can assist the chef throughout his or her career. This is truly an encyclopedic work, based on years of professional and teaching experience. To all who are endeavoring to learn the art of French pastry making, as either a professional or a serious amateur, I offer my best wishes for success. It is a wonderful and rewarding experience.

MARKUS FARBINGER
Executive Pastry Chef
Le Cirque Restaurant
New York

When pastry chefs come upon a new book about their craft, their first response is to look for new recipes that can improve their work and inspiring photographs that will enable the creation of more innovative products. The *Professional French Pastry Series* provides both. More important, however, it includes material essential to the day-to-day work of the pastry chef: information about raw ingredients, without which there would be no creation; new and traditional techniques for both making and using pastry; and a historical look at pastry products that enables us to recognize and be a part of the traditions of French pastry making.

In my position as a teacher, I have found this series to be a precious helper; in my position as a chef, an indispensable working tool.

JEAN-MARIE GUICHARD
Director of Instruction
Cacao Barry Training Center
Pennsauken, New Jersey

Photography crédits
The photographs in the book
are from Pierre Michalet

First published as *Traité de pâtisserie artisanale - Décor, Bordures et
lettres, Modelage pate d'amandes, Nouveaux entremets, Pièces de prestige*
by Editions St-Honoré, Paris, France; copyright © 1987.

Second edition (English)
Printed in E.E.C. by
Interlitho (Milano)
First Quarter - 1998
A copublication

and

**WILEY**

ISBN 0 470 25000 3

**John Wiley & Sons, Inc.**
Professional, Reference and Trade Group
605 Third Avenue, New York, N.Y. 10158-0012
New York • Chichester • Bribane • Toronto • Singapore

ISBN 0 442 20569 4

**CICEM** (Compagnie Internationale
de Consultation *Education* et *Media*)
23 Bd Henri IV 75004 Paris